Photoshop - Touch-Up And Image Adjustments

Supports Photoshop CC, CS6, and Mac Versions

In this workbook, we will first review core concepts from the Level 1 book, as well as engage in an in-depth discussion of the most commonly used **Drawing Tools**. Healing, Correction, and Clone Stamping, which are tools used to fix problems on an image, will also be covered. Furthermore, a better understanding of the **Layers Panel** will allow you to keep track of various layers such as text, drawings, and smart objects. **Image Adjustment** techniques, such as how to brighten photos, change contrast, balance colors, change exposure, highlight colors, and create photo filters will also be discussed. We will also cover techniques to mask objects, warp text, as well as other special effects techniques. A few advanced features such as actions, batch, video editing, and editing 3D objects will also be introduced. Being able to use a combination of commands will invite you to new possibilities that can be generated to develop new enhancing skills. Command differences are provided for **Photoshop CS6, CC,** and **Mac CS6**.

Copyright and Release Information

This workbook/guide was updated on **1/4/2023 (Version 4)** and is designed for **Adobe Photoshop CC** and **CS6**. Also, **Mac CS6** commands have been added due to keyboard and menu differences. This guide is the sole property of Jeff Hutchinson and **eLearnLogic.** Any emailing, copying, duplication, or reproduction of this guide, must be approved by Jeff Hutchinson in writing. However, students who take a class or purchase the guide are free to use it for personal development and learning.
ISBN-13: 978-1976401602, ISBN-10: 1976401607.

Exercise Download

Exercises are posted on the website and can be downloaded to your computer.
Please do the following:
Open Internet Explorer.   Or Google Chrome:

Type the web address: **elearnlogic.com/download/photoshopcc-2.exe**
You might get several security warnings, but answer yes and run through each one. When you click "**Unzip,**" the files will be located in **C:\Data\PhotoshopCC-2** folder.

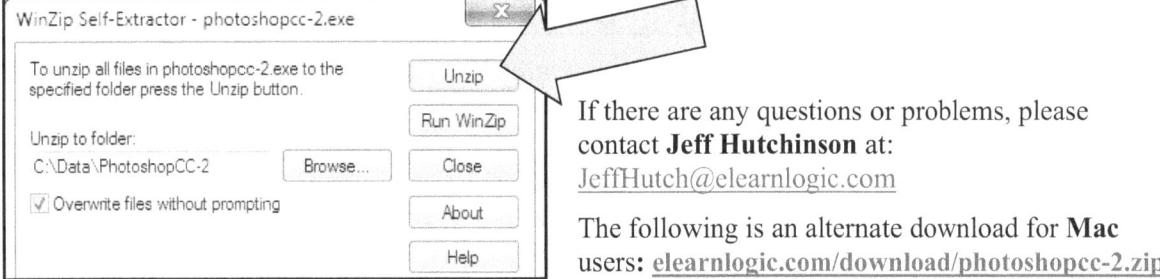

If there are any questions or problems, please contact **Jeff Hutchinson** at:
JeffHutch@elearnlogic.com

The following is an alternate download for **Mac** users: elearnlogic.com/download/photoshopcc-2.zip

Introduction

About the Author

Jeff Hutchinson is a computer instructor teaching a variety of classes around the country. He has a BS degree from BYU in Computer-Aided Engineering and has worked in the Information Technology field supporting and maintaining computers for many years. He also previously owned a computer training and consulting firm in San Francisco, California. After selling his business in 2001, he continued to work as an independent computer instructor/consultant around the country. Jeff Hutchinson lives in Utah and also provides training for Utah Valley University Community Education system, offering valuable computer skills for the general knowledge of students, career development, and career advancement. Understanding the technology and the needs of students has been the basis for developing this material. Jeff Hutchinson can be contacted at jeffhutch@elearnlogic.com or (801) 376-6687.

Design Strategy

This workbook is designed in conjunction with an Online-Instructor-Led course (for more information see: www.elearnlogic.com). Unlike other computer guides, students will not need to review lengthy procedures in order to understand a topic. All that is necessary are the brief statements and command paths located within the guide that demonstrate how a concept is used. There are many **Step-By-Step Practice Exercises** and more comprehensive **Student Projects** used to better understand a concept. Furthermore, students will find that this workbook guide is often used as a reference to help users understand concepts quickly. An **Index** and a **Detailed Table Of Contents** are also provided on the last few pages of the workbook to reference important topics as necessary. However, if more detail is needed for study, the Internet can be used to search for a concept. Also, if students' skills are weak due to lack of use, they can refresh their knowledge quickly by visually scanning the concept needed and then testing them out using the application.

Manual Organization

The following are special formatting conventions:

- **Numbered Sections** on the left are the **Concepts** covered.
- *Italic Text* is used to highlight commands that will perform the **Concept** or procedure in completing the practice exercises.
- **Practice Exercises** are a **Step-by-Step** approach to demonstrating the **Concept.**
- **Student Projects** are a more comprehensive approach to demonstrating the **Concept.**
- **Bolded** items are important **Concepts,** terminology, or commands used.
- **Tip** - These are additional ideas about a Concept.
- **CS5+** - The statement indicates the concept was added to **Photoshop CS5**.

Obtain Your PDF Copy and Video Course

To obtain a **PDF** copy of the workbook and a link to an **Online Recorded Video Course,** send an email to jeffhutch@elearnlogic.com along with your Amazon receipt/confirmation. To see an example clip and a list of **Remote Online Courses** available worldwide, go to www.elearnlogic.com.

Table of Contents

Chapter 1 - Quick Review **5**
Chapter 2 - In-Depth Drawing Tools **8**
   Section 1: Core Tools..8
   Section 2: Optional Tools 21
Chapter 3 - Touch-Up Images **35**
Chapter 4 - Advanced Layers **47**
   Section 1: Layer Panel Options..47
   Section 2: Visible Layers 50
   Section 3: Layer Menu...53
   Section 4: Layer Manipulation...54
Chapter 5 - Image Adjustments...**55**
   Section 1: Canvas and Image Size Adjustments..55
   Section 2: Image Adjustments 59
   Section 3: Color Adjustments 64
   Section 4: Color Replacement Adjustment 69
   Section 5: Toning Adjustments..71
   Section 6: Other Color Adjustments..73
Chapter 6 - Masking Capabilities...**77**
   Section 1: Select and Mask 77
   Section 2: Quick Mask 81
   Section 3: Layer Mask 82
   Section 4: Clipping Mask 84
   Section 5: Advanced Techniques 86
Chapter 7 - Text Layer Effects **89**
   Section 1: Text Formatting...89
   Section 2: Reshape Text Path 91
   Section 3: Layer Comps...94
   Section 4: Vanishing Point 95
Chapter 8 - Advanced Features **97**
   Section 1: Neural Filters 97
   Section 2: Actions 107
   Section 3: Video Editing..109
   Section 4: 3D Object Manipulation 115
Index - Touch-Up And Image Adjustments **117**
Detailed Table Of Contents..**118**

Chapter 1 - Quick Review

A quick review of the fundamental concepts of **Photoshop** will lay the foundation for this course.

1.1 Exercises

Exercise files on **PC** are located in **C:\Data\PhotoshopCC-2** folder, and the **Mac** is usually stored in the download folder. Refer to the exercise download instructions on page 1

Practice Exercise 1 - Open Countryside.jpg

Use the following file to test the capabilities of this chapter:

File Menu→Open→C:\Data\PhotoshopCC-2\Countryside.jpg→ `Open` .
Tip: If you make changes, do not save the file using the same name.

1.2 Mac Keyboard Commands

There are a few fundamental differences to identify between the Mac and PC:

`Ctrl` *key (Windows)* = `Command` *key (Mac).*
`Alt` *key (Windows)* = `Option` *key (Mac).*
Edit Menu→Preferences (Windows)** = **Photoshop Menu→Preferences (Mac).

1.3 Photoshop Environment

This includes **Tools**, **Options**, **Menus**, **Panels**, **Status,** and **Document** windows.

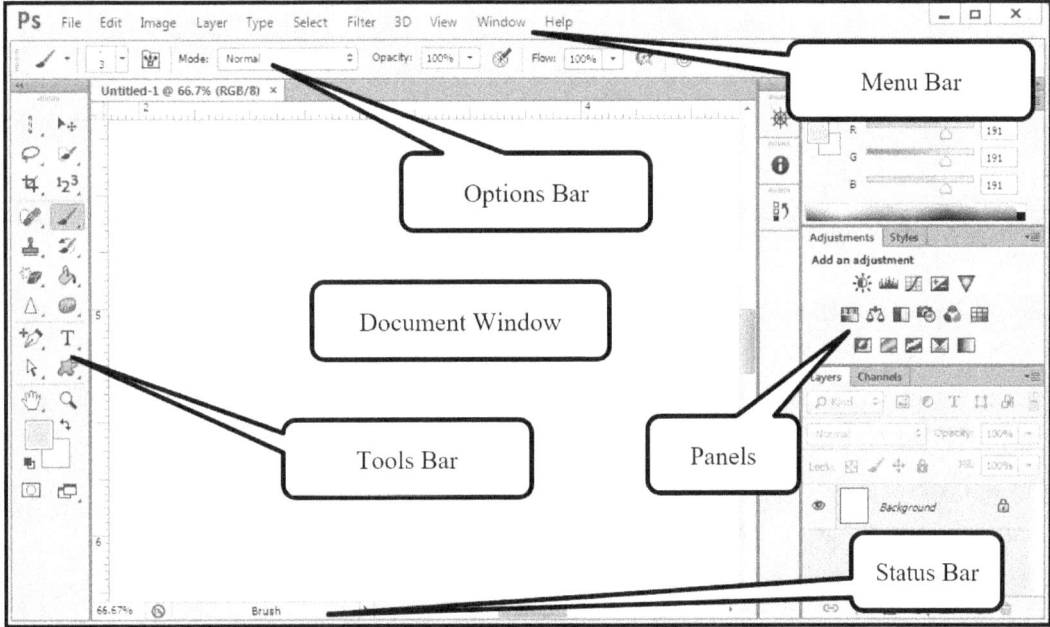

1.4 Zooming

There are a variety of **Zooming Tools** available:

Zoom In: 🔍*Zoom Tool→Click on the work area.*
Zoom Out: 🔍 *Zoom Tool→Hold* `Alt` *key→Click on the work area.*
Mac CS6: *Use the* `Option` `Spacebar` *keys instead of the* `Alt` *key.*
Keyboard: `Ctrl` `+` , `Ctrl` `-` , `Ctrl` `1` , and `Ctrl` `0` keys.

Page 5

Mac CS6: *Use the* Command *key.*
Special: Hold the: Ctrl Spacebar *keys and click on the work area.*
Hold the: Ctrl Alt Spacebar *keys and click on the work area.*
Mac CS6: *Use the* Command Spacebar *and* Option Command Spacebar *key combinations.*

1.5 Panels

The following commonly used **Panels** can be added using **Window Menu** and are located on the right side of the screen.
Color, Swatches, Stroke, Layers, History, Info, and Navigator.

1.6 Basic Drawing Tools

These are the most commonly used tools:

Brush Tool	Eraser Tool	Paint Bucket Tool
Pencil Tool	Hand Tool	Horizontal Type Tool
Move Tool	Eye Dropper Tool	

1.7 Resolution Type

This includes **Vector** vs **Raster** graphics, **Image size (Image Menu→Image Size)**, **Canvas size (Image Menu→Canvas Size)**, **RGB**, and **CMYK**.

1.8 Selection

These are the most commonly used **Selection Tools**:

Rectangular Marquee Tool	Lasso Tool	Quick Selection Tool
Elliptical Marquee Tool	Polygon Selection Tool	Magic Wand Tool
	Magnetic Lasso Tool	Object Selection Tool

1.9 Layers

The following are a few **Layer** related concepts:
Background Layer , **Blank Layer** , Move Layer to File, Create layer from selection, **Type layers** , New group, arrange layers, Transform layers, Free Transform, Merge and Flatten layers.

1.10 Filter Effects

The following are a few **Filter Effects**:
Filter Menu, Filter Gallery, Blur, Distort, noise, etc.

1.11 Layer Effects

The following are a few **Layer Effects**:
Opacity/Transparency, Blending modes, Bevel/Emboss, etc.

1.12 Saving Techniques

File Menu →Save As →Filename: C:\Data\PhotoshopCC-2\Countryside1

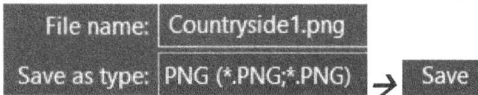 → Save

Chapter 1 - Quick Review

File Menu→Export→(Choose JPG, PNG, or GIF).

1.13 Duplicate Layers

The following are a couple of ways to make a copy of a **Layer**:
Right-click on Layer→Duplicate
Ctrl J (Command J mac)
Drag layer to ⊞ New Layer (located on the bottom of the Layers Panel).

1.14 Help Tools

If you can't find a command or tool: *Click 🔍 icon (located in the upper right corner)→Type a tool name (like clone)→ Select the Tool.*

1.15 Color Picker

The **Color Picker** is located at the bottom of the **Tools Panel** (left side of the interface) and is used to define the **Foreground** and **Background** colors. The **Foreground** color (color on top) is the default color used for tools such as **Paint Bucket** or **Paint Brush Tools**. The following will describe some of the icons located in the **Color Picker**:

Default Background and Foreground Colors - By clicking on this button, the **Foreground** color will be set to black and the **Background** color will turn white.

Switch Background and Foreground Color - When this button is pressed, the **Foreground** and **Background** color are **Switched** in order to draw with the default color.

Foreground and Background Color - The box on top contains the **Foreground** color and is also the default color used by the system. The box under the **Foreground** is the **Background** color available if you use the **Switch** button.

Foreground Color Picker - This will open the **Foreground Color Picker** dialog box that defines color.

In order to choose a different color: *Double click on the Foreground box in the Color Picker (located at the bottom of the Tools Panel).*

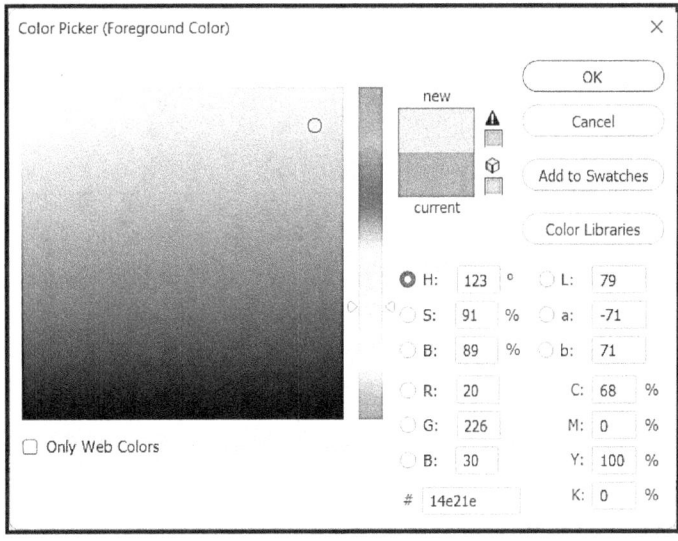

Chapter 2 - In-Depth Drawing Tools

In this chapter, we will cover **Drawing Tools** as well as many related **Options**.

Chapter Contents:

Section 1: Tools - This will include the **Tools:** Move, Eye Dropper, Brush, Pencil, History Brush, Eraser, Paint Bucket, Horizontal Type, Shape, and Hand Tools.

Section 2: Optional Concepts - This will include the **Tools**: Color Replacement, Mixer Brush, Background Eraser, Color Sampler, Art History Brush, Gradient, Pattern Stamp, Create Custom Patterns, Ruler, Note, Count, Magic Eraser, Slice, Slice Select, Brush Defaults, Add New Brushes, and Create New Brushes.

Section 1: Core Tools

Here, we will cover the **Core Tools** used and the **Options Panel** in great detail. The following is an example of the **Paint Brush Options Panel**:

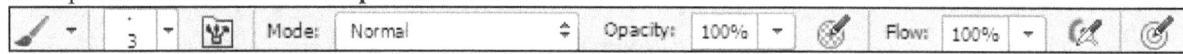

Section Table Of Contents:

2.1 Move Tool	2.5 History Brush Tool	2.9 Shape Tools
2.2 Eye Dropper Tool	2.6 Eraser Tool	2.10 Hand Tool
2.3 Brush Tool	2.7 Paint Bucket Tool	
2.4 Pencil Tool	2.8 Horizontal Type Tool	

2.1 Move Tool

The **Move Tool** is used to **Move** an image on a layer as well as an entire document to a different location on a document or an entirely different document.

2.1-1 There are several ways to use the **Move Tool**:

1. **Move a selected area to another location on one document:** *Rectangular Marquee Tool → Draw Rectangle → Select the Move Tool → Move the selected area.*

2. **Move a Layer to a different document:** *Open 2 documents → Window Menu → Arrange → Tile All Vertically → Select Layer → Select the Move Tool → Move the selected area to a different document.*

3. **Move the entire document to another document:** *Open 2 documents → Window Menu → Arrange → Tile All Vertically → Select all Layers using the* Ctrl *or* Shift *keys → Select the Move Tool → Move all layers to a different document.*

2.1-2 Move Tool Options

The following are the **Move Tool** options located just under **Menus** on top of the interface:

Preset Picker - This will allow you to quickly access a tool that has been predefined. To save the current **Move Tool** settings, press and quickly access the **Move Tool.**

Auto-Select - This will select the **Layer** or **Group** when you click on the object. If unchecked, it will not select an **Object** or **Layer**.

Layer or Group - If you have no **Groups**, then choose the **Layer** option.

Chapter 2 - In-Depth Drawing Tools

Show Transform Controls - This will show the **Transform Controls** on a selected object. Example:

Align options

    Vertical Alignment - This will **Align** selected objects placed in different layers **Vertically.**

    Horizontal Alignment - This will **Align** selected objects placed in different layers **Horizontally.**

    Distribute - This will **Distribute** objects placed in different layers **Vertically** or **Horizontally**.

    Distribute Spacing - This will evenly space objects placed on different layers **Vertically** or **Horizontally**.

Align To - This will **Align** the **Canvas** to a selected object. If you select an area in the middle of an image using the **Rectangle Selection Tool**, a **Canvas** will **Align To** the selection by using the **Alignment Tools** above.

Practice Exercise 2 - Move to file

1. *File Menu→Open→C:\Data\PhotoshopCC-2\Backdrop.jpg→* Open .
2. *File Menu→Open→C:\Data\PhotoshopCC-2\Logo.png →* Open .
3. *Window Menu→Arrange →* Tile All Vertically .
4. *Select the Move Tool →Move the logo to the backdrop.*

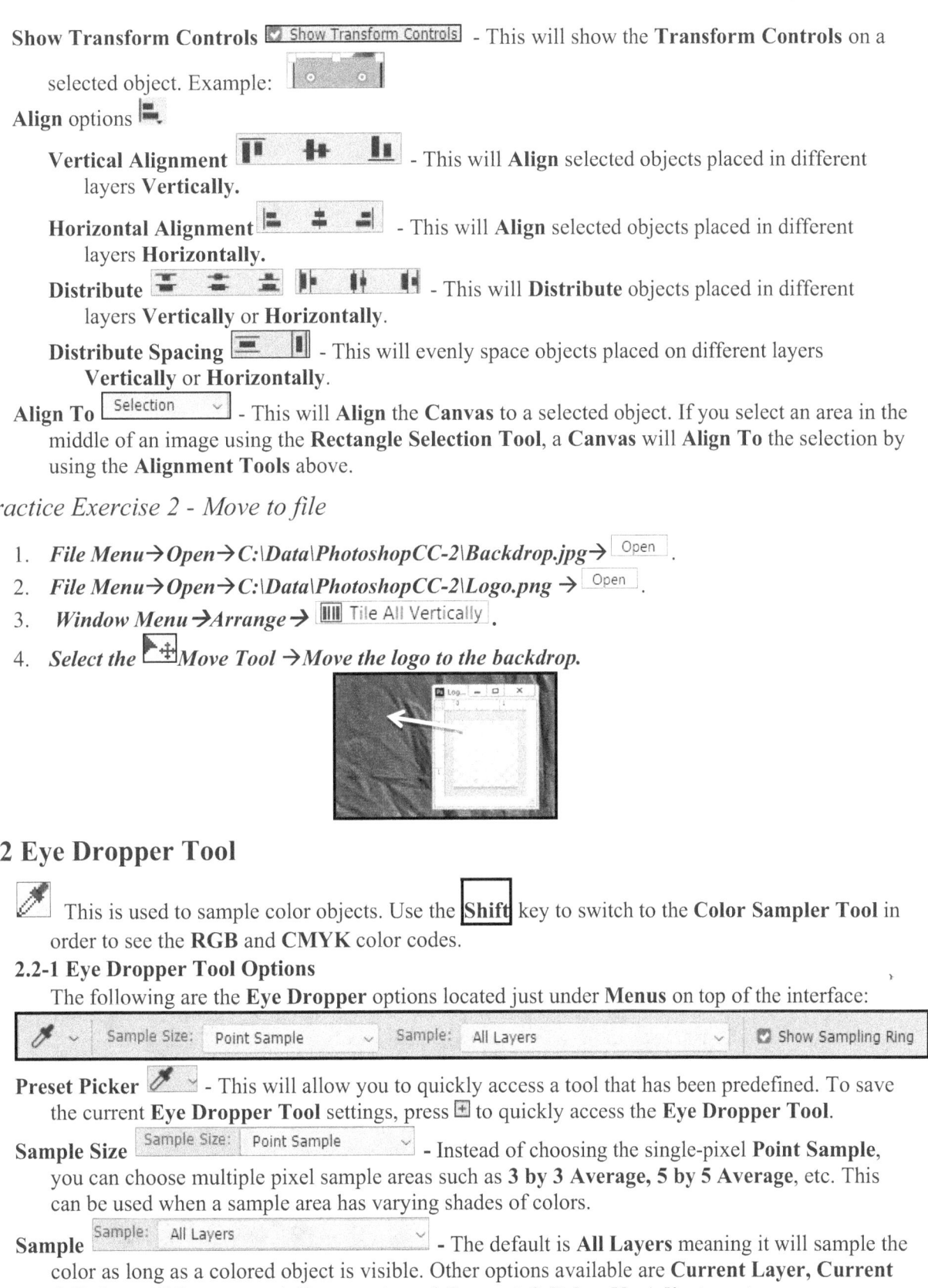

2.2 Eye Dropper Tool

This is used to sample color objects. Use the **Shift** key to switch to the **Color Sampler Tool** in order to see the **RGB** and **CMYK** color codes.

2.2-1 Eye Dropper Tool Options

The following are the **Eye Dropper** options located just under **Menus** on top of the interface:

Preset Picker - This will allow you to quickly access a tool that has been predefined. To save the current **Eye Dropper Tool** settings, press to quickly access the **Eye Dropper Tool**.

Sample Size - Instead of choosing the single-pixel **Point Sample**, you can choose multiple pixel sample areas such as **3 by 3 Average, 5 by 5 Average**, etc. This can be used when a sample area has varying shades of colors.

Sample - The default is **All Layers** meaning it will sample the color as long as a colored object is visible. Other options available are **Current Layer, Current & Below, All Layers no Adjustments,** and **Current & Below No Adjustments.**

Show Sampling Ring - When sampled, you will see a large ring around the area.

Chapter 2 - In-Depth Drawing Tools

Practice Exercise 3 - Eye Dropper

File Menu→Open→C:\Data\PhotoshopCC-2\Balloons.jpg→ Open .
Select the Eyedropper Tool→Sample the color desired (Alt *Click)→Create a swatch: Swatches Panel→Click Create New Swatch or use a Brush Tool to paint the color.*

Practice Exercise 4 - Eye Dropper Sample Size

1. *File Menu→Open→C:\Data\PhotoshopCC-2\Beach.jpg→* Open .
2. *Zoom into a distant boat→Eyedropper Tool→Eyedropper options Sample Size: 3 by 3 Average→ Hold the* Alt *key and take 3 samples in the water near the boat.*
   Mac CS6: *Use the* option *key.*
3. *Sample the water: Click→Click→Click.*
4. *Use the Brush Tool to paint the sampled color over the boat→Brush Size: 5→ Make sure the color picker is set to the blue water sample.*

2.3 Brush Tool

This draws freehand using different brush types.

2.3-1 The following decisions must be considered prior to using the **Brush Tool:**

1. **Change the Brush Color in the Color Picker:** *(located at the bottom of the Tools).*

2. **Add additional Brushes:** *Brush options →Brush Preset Picker dropdown → Brush Preset Picker Menu (top Right side) to choose additional brush Styles such as Append Default Brushes or Legacy Brushes.*

3. **Cursor Style -** Press the Caps Lock key to change the **Cursor** to a more precise drawing layout.
   Caps Lock/off is a circle and **Caps Lock/on** is a cross with a dot.

2.3-2 Brush Tool Options

The following are the **Brush Tool** options located just under **Menus** on top of the interface:

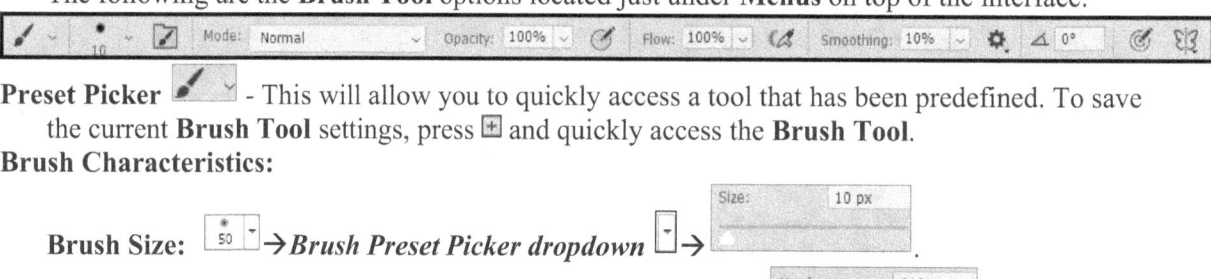

Preset Picker - This will allow you to quickly access a tool that has been predefined. To save the current **Brush Tool** settings, press and quickly access the **Brush Tool**.

Brush Characteristics:

Brush Size: →*Brush Preset Picker dropdown →*

Brush Hardness: →*Brush Preset Picker dropdown →*

Brushes: →*Brush Preset Picker dropdown →*

Brush Settings Panel or - This will toggle the **Brush Settings Panel**.

Chapter 2 - In-Depth Drawing Tools

Painting Mode `Mode: Normal` - Oftentimes, a **Mode** will blend with colors behind the stroke. The most commonly used **Modes** are **Color Burn, Linear Dodge, Vivid Light, Linear Light, Hard Mix,** and **Difference.**

Opacity 100% `Opacity: 100%` - The **Brush Stroke** is more see-through or transparent. Solid is 100%, 0% is see-through, and 20% is visible but partially see-through.

Pressure for Opacity - **Opacity** will change depending on the amount of pressure applied using a tablet pen (not a mouse). When turned off, **Brush Preset** controls pressure.

Flow `Flow: 100%` - This is a percentage that sets the rate of color applied or the amount of ink that is applied to the tool.

Airbrush - This simulates painting with an **Airbrush.**

Smoothing `Smoothing: 10%` - This will **Smooth** the **Stroke** (border) edges. A higher value will make a **Stroke Smoother** as you draw.

Brush Smoothing Options - This will adjust the **Smoothing** options such as **Pulled String Mode, Stroke Catch-up, Catch-up on Stroke End,** and **Adjust for Zoom.**

Brush Angle `0°` - This will set the **Angle** when you begin to draw. It is not noticeable in normal situations.

Pressure For Size - Always use **Pressure For Size**. When turned off, **Brush Preset** controls pressure. This works best with a tablet pen rather than a mouse.

Symmetry Options - This will define a specific path to use a **Brush Tool**.

Practice Exercise 5 - Brush Tool

File Menu →New →Print Tab → Print Presets →Letter (8.5 x 11 in @ 300 ppi → `Create`.

Draw with a color Light Blue →Draw a vertical line using `Mode: Normal` *→Draw horizontal crossing lines using Normal, Multiply, Hard Light, and Hard Mix →Inspect the differences.*

When finished, switch back to `Mode: Normal`.

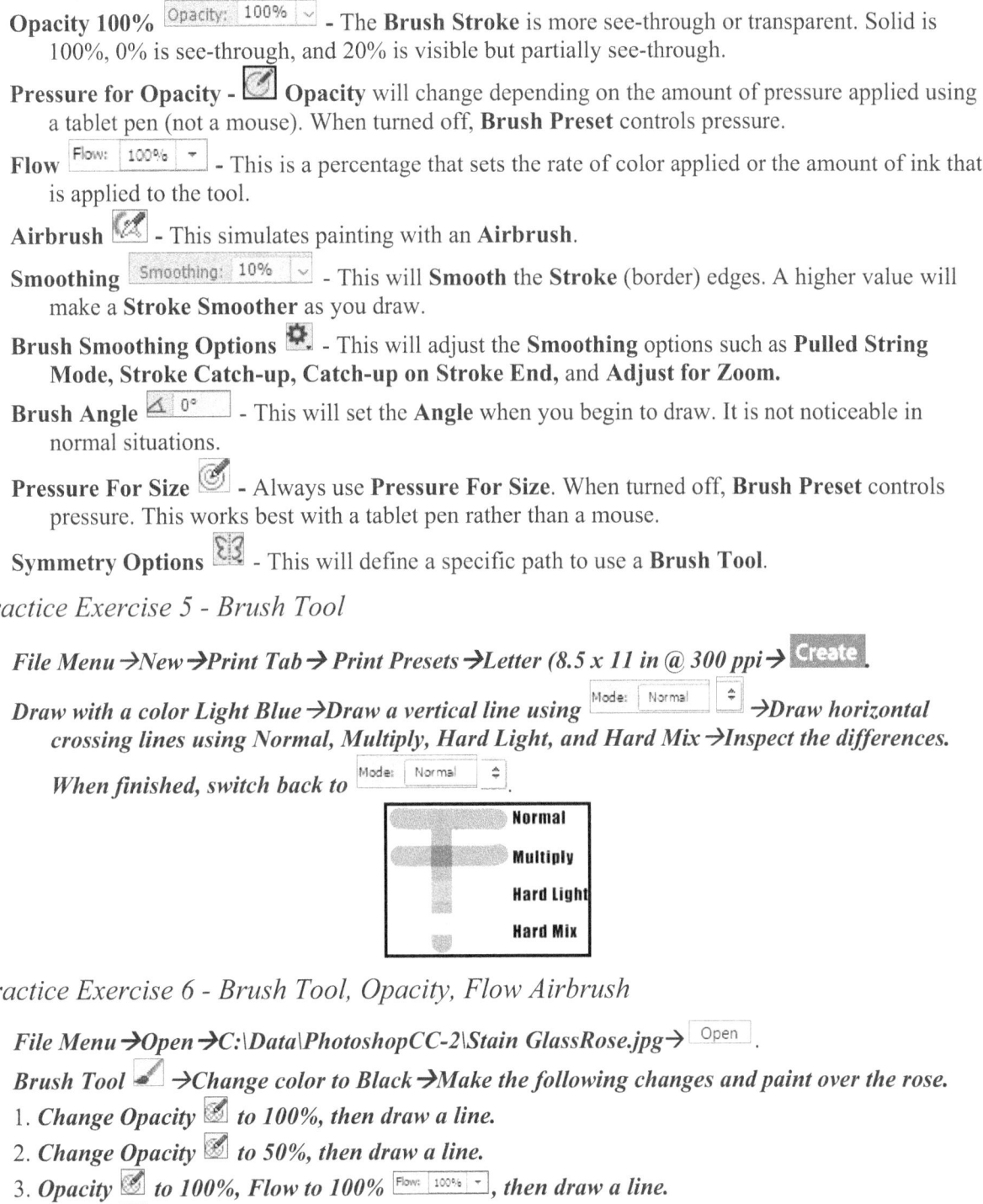

Practice Exercise 6 - Brush Tool, Opacity, Flow Airbrush

File Menu →Open →C:\Data\PhotoshopCC-2\Stain GlassRose.jpg → `Open`.

Brush Tool →Change color to Black →Make the following changes and paint over the rose.

1. Change Opacity to 100%, then draw a line.

2. Change Opacity to 50%, then draw a line.

3. Opacity to 100%, Flow to 100% `Flow: 100%`*, then draw a line.*

4. Opacity to 100%, Flow to 50% `Flow: 100%`*, then draw a line.*

5. It is difficult to see the results of the Airbrush .

6. The Pressure For Size will only work with a special mouse or pen.

7. Zoom in to see the differences.

2.4 Pencil Tool

This draws free hand. Hold the **Shift** key to draw continuous line segments. *Select the Pencil Tool → Click, Click, Click.*

2.4-1 The following decisions must be considered prior to using the **Pencil Tool**:

1. **Change the Pencil Color in the Color Picker:** *(located on the bottom of the Tools).*
2. **Add additional Brushes:** *Brush options → Brush Preset Picker dropdown → Brush Preset Picker Menu (top Right side) to choose additional brush Styles such as Append Default Brushes or Legacy Brushes.*
3. **Cursor Style** - Press the **Caps Lock** key to change the **Cursor** to a more precise drawing layout. **Caps Lock/off** is a circle and **Caps Lock/on** is a cross with a dot.

2.4-2 Pencil Tool Options

The following are the **Pencil Tool** options located just under **Menus** on top of the interface:

Preset Picker - This will allow you to quickly access a tool that has been predefined. To save the current **Pencil Tool** settings, press and quickly access the **Pencil Tool.**

Pencil Characteristics:

Brush Size: *→ Brush Preset Picker dropdown →*

Brush Hardness: *→ Brush Preset Picker dropdown →*

Brushes: *→ Brush Preset Picker dropdown →*

Brush Settings Panel - This will toggle the **Brush Settings Panel.**

Painting Mode - Oftentimes, the **Mode** will blend with colors behind the stroke. The most commonly used **Modes** are **Color Burn, Linear Dodge, Vivid Light, Linear Light, Hard Mix,** and **Difference**.

Opacity 100% - The **Brush Stroke** is more see-through or transparent. Solid is 100%, 0% is see-through, and 20% is visible but partially see-through.

Pressure for Opacity - The **Opacity** will change depending on the amount of pressure applied using a tablet pen (not a mouse). When turned off, **Brush Preset** controls pressure.

Flow - This is a percentage that sets the rate of color applied or the amount of ink that is applied to the tool.

Smoothing - This will **Smooth** the **Stroke** (border) edges. A higher value will make the **Stroke Smoother** as you draw.

Pencil Smoothing Options - This will adjust the **Smoothing** options such as **Pulled String Mode, Stroke Catch-up, Catch-up on Stroke End,** and **Adjust for Zoom.**

Chapter 2 - In-Depth Drawing Tools

Pencil Angle - This will set an **Angle** as you begin to draw. However, this is not noticeable in normal situations.

Auto Erase - When checked ✓, this paints the background color over the foreground color. It only draws the background when you begin drawing on top of a previous **Pencil** segment with the foreground color.

Pressure For Size - Always use **Pressure For Size**. When turned off, **Brush Preset** controls **Pressure**. This works best with a tablet pen rather than a mouse.

Symmetry Options - This will define a specific path using the **Pencil Tool**.

Practice Exercise 7 - Auto Erase

1. *File Menu→New→Print Tab→ Print Presets→Letter (8.5 x 11 in @ 300 ppi)→Background Contents: White→ Create.*
2. *Make sure your color picker has color in the foreground and white in the background.*
3. *Pencil Tool→UnCheck Auto Erase →Draw several lines.*
4. *Pencil Tool→Check Auto Erase →Draw several lines.*

   Tip: When you draw lines on top of each other, you are drawing the background color.

2.5 History Brush Tool

This offers more control over the **Undo** feature. It allows you to return specific areas within an image to a prior state while the rest of the image remains unchanged. *Window Menu→History.*

2.5-1 The following decisions must be considered prior to using the **History Brush Tool**:

1. **Change the History Brush Color in the Color Picker:** *(located at the bottom of the Tools).*
2. **Add additional Brushes:** *Brush options →Brush Preset Picker dropdown → Brush Preset Picker Menu (top Right side) to choose additional brush Styles such as Append Default Brushes or Legacy Brushes.*
3. **Cursor Style -** Press the Caps Lock key to change the **Cursor** to a more precise drawing layout. **Caps Lock/off** is a circle ○ and **Caps Lock/on** is a cross with a dot.

2.5-2 The following are the **History Brush Tool** options located just under **Menus** on the top of interface:

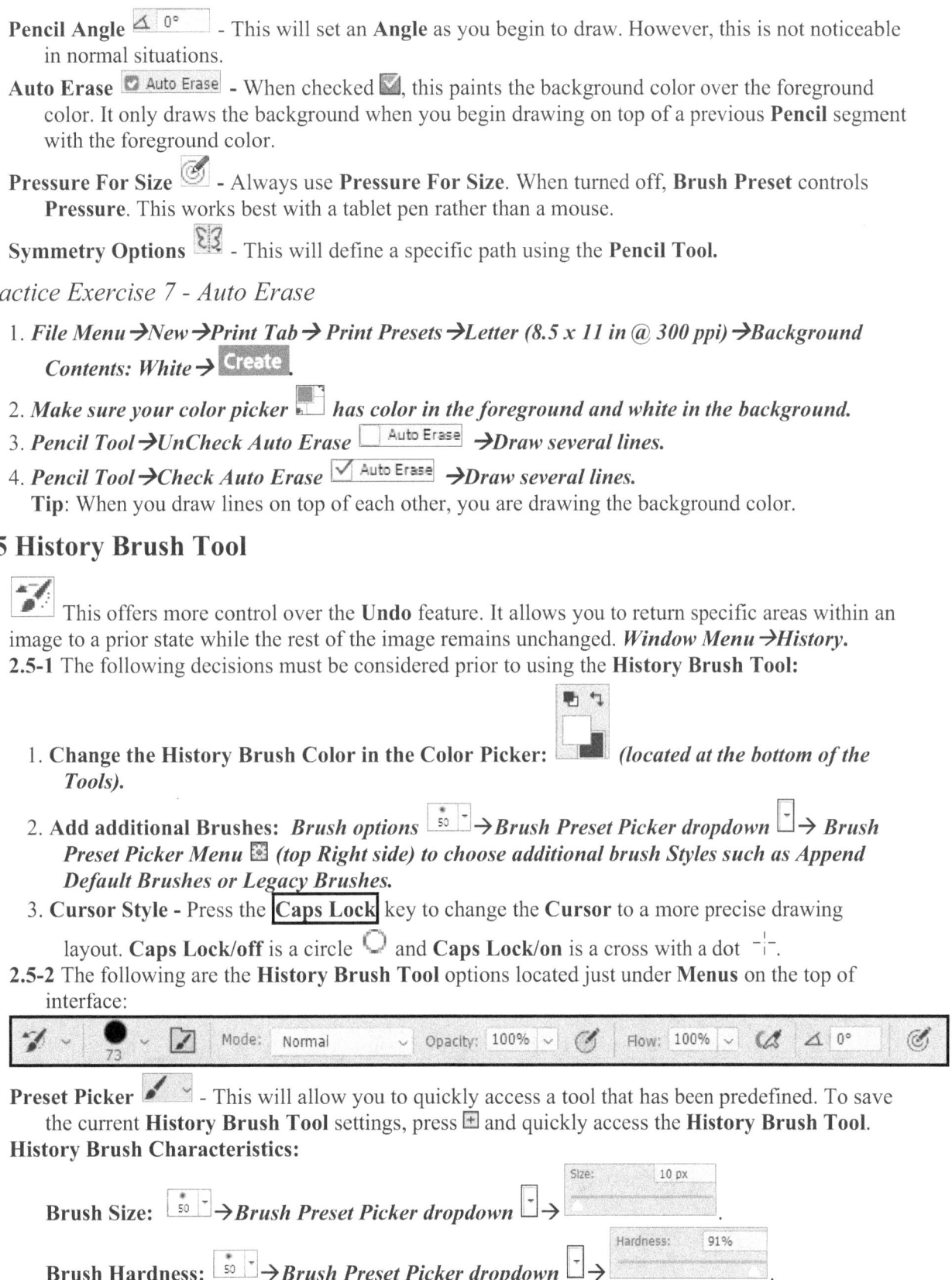

Preset Picker - This will allow you to quickly access a tool that has been predefined. To save the current **History Brush Tool** settings, press ⊞ and quickly access the **History Brush Tool**.

History Brush Characteristics:

Brush Size: →*Brush Preset Picker dropdown* →.

Brush Hardness: →*Brush Preset Picker dropdown* →.

Chapter 2 - In-Depth Drawing Tools

Brushes: →*Brush Preset Picker dropdown* → .

Brush Settings Panel or - This will toggle the **Brush Settings Panel**.

Painting Mode - Oftentimes, the **Mode** will blend with the colors behind a stroke. The most commonly used **Modes** are **Color Burn, Linear Dodge, Vivid Light, Linear Light, Hard Mix,** and **Difference**.

Opacity 100% - The **Brush Stroke** is more see-through or transparent. Solid is 100%, 0% is see-through, and 20% is visible but partially see-through.

Pressure for Opacity - The **Opacity** will change depending on the amount of **Pressure** applied using a tablet pen (not a mouse). When turned off, **Brush Preset** controls **Pressure**.

Flow - This is a percentage that sets the rate of color applied or the amount of ink that is applied to the tool.

Airbrush - This simulates painting with an **Airbrush**.

Brush Angle - This will set the **Angle** when you begin to draw. It is not noticeable in normal situations.

Pressure For Size - This will always use **Pressure For Size**. When turned off, **Brush Preset** controls **Pressure**. This works best with a tablet pen rather than a mouse.

Practice Exercise 8 - History Brush

1. *File Menu→Open→C:\Data\PhotoshopCC-2\Boy.jpg→* .
2. *Filter Menu→Blur→Gaussian Blur→Radius: 5→* .
3. *Window Menu→History Panel→Check the History Brush icon in front of the open in the History Panel, for example:*
4. *History Brush Tool →Paint over the boy's face using the History Brush Tool.*

2.6 Eraser Tool

 This is used to **Erase** objects, colors, and lines in the foreground down to the default color of a background. To change the size of the **Eraser** area, choose the following dropdown located in the tool options. If you select an area it will only **Erase** that selected area.

2.6-1 Eraser Tool Options

The following are the **Eraser Tool** options located just under **Menus** on top of the interface:

Preset Picker - This will allow you to quickly access a tool that has been predefined. To save the current **Eraser Tool** settings, press and quickly access the **Eraser Tool**.

Eraser Tool Characteristics:

Brush Size: →*Brush Preset Picker dropdown* → .

Brush Hardness: →*Brush Preset Picker dropdown* → .

Chapter 2 - In-Depth Drawing Tools

Brushes: →*Brush Preset Picker dropdown* → 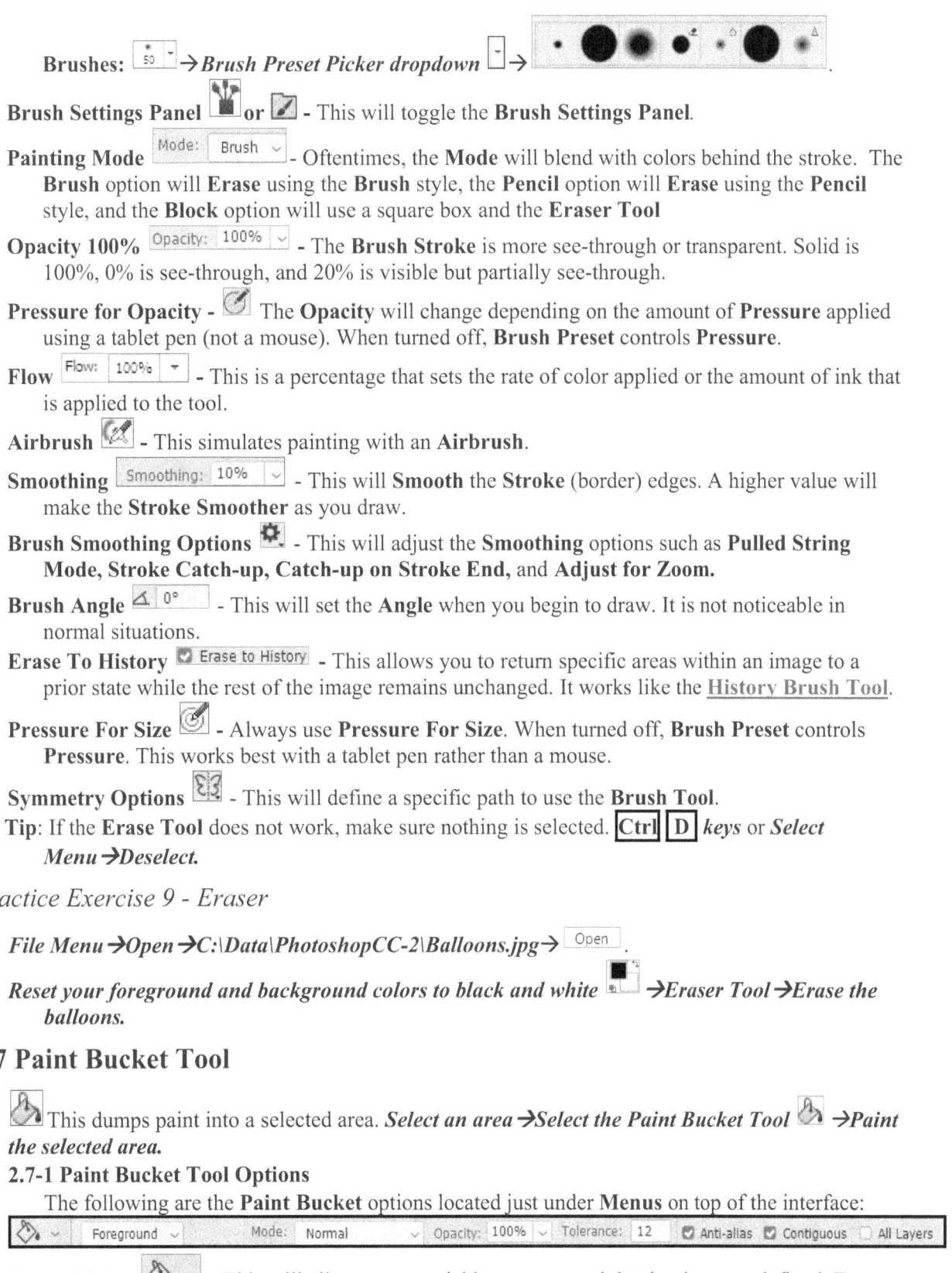.

Brush Settings Panel or - This will toggle the **Brush Settings Panel**.

Painting Mode - Oftentimes, the **Mode** will blend with colors behind the stroke. The **Brush** option will **Erase** using the **Brush** style, the **Pencil** option will **Erase** using the **Pencil** style, and the **Block** option will use a square box and the **Eraser Tool**

Opacity 100% - The **Brush Stroke** is more see-through or transparent. Solid is 100%, 0% is see-through, and 20% is visible but partially see-through.

Pressure for Opacity - The **Opacity** will change depending on the amount of **Pressure** applied using a tablet pen (not a mouse). When turned off, **Brush Preset** controls **Pressure**.

Flow - This is a percentage that sets the rate of color applied or the amount of ink that is applied to the tool.

Airbrush - This simulates painting with an **Airbrush**.

Smoothing - This will **Smooth** the **Stroke** (border) edges. A higher value will make the **Stroke Smoother** as you draw.

Brush Smoothing Options - This will adjust the **Smoothing** options such as **Pulled String Mode, Stroke Catch-up, Catch-up on Stroke End,** and **Adjust for Zoom.**

Brush Angle - This will set the **Angle** when you begin to draw. It is not noticeable in normal situations.

Erase To History - This allows you to return specific areas within an image to a prior state while the rest of the image remains unchanged. It works like the History Brush Tool.

Pressure For Size - Always use **Pressure For Size**. When turned off, **Brush Preset** controls **Pressure**. This works best with a tablet pen rather than a mouse.

Symmetry Options - This will define a specific path to use the **Brush Tool**.

Tip: If the **Erase Tool** does not work, make sure nothing is selected. **Ctrl** **D** *keys* or *Select Menu→Deselect.*

Practice Exercise 9 - Eraser

File Menu→Open→C:\Data\PhotoshopCC-2\Balloons.jpg→

Reset your foreground and background colors to black and white →Eraser Tool→Erase the balloons.

2.7 Paint Bucket Tool

This dumps paint into a selected area. ***Select an area →Select the Paint Bucket Tool →Paint the selected area.***

2.7-1 Paint Bucket Tool Options

The following are the **Paint Bucket** options located just under **Menus** on top of the interface:

Preset Picker - This will allow you to quickly access a tool that has been predefined. To save the current **Paint Bucket Tool** settings, press and quickly access the **Paint Bucket Tool**.

Chapter 2 - In-Depth Drawing Tools

Foreground `Foreground` `Pattern` - This sets the fill area and **Foreground**. The other option is

Painting Mode `Mode: Normal` - Oftentimes, the **Mode** will blend with colors behind the **Stroke**. The most commonly used **Modes** are **Color Burn, Linear Dodge, Vivid Light, Linear Light, Hard Mix,** and **Difference**.

Opacity 100% `Opacity: 100%` - The **Brush Stroke** is more see-through or transparent. Solid is 100%, 0% is see-through, and 20% is visible but partially see-through.

Tolerance `Tolerance: 32` - This defines the sensitivity to color differences or more pixels with similar colors. **Default=32**. A higher number will select more of the object with a slightly different color range and a lower number will be less **Tolerant** of color differences.

Anti-Alias ☑ Anti-alias If checked, this will smooth the hard or jagged edges of a selection. When unchecked, selections will appear more jagged. In some cases, this option will be disabled, but it will default to the checked **Anti-alias** state.

Contiguous ☑ Contiguous - This will sample pixels that complete a circular selection.

All Layers ☑ All Layers - This creates a selection considering **All Layers**.

2.8 Horizontal Type Tool

To type text on a **New Layer,** use the **Horizontal Type Tool**. Other **Text (Type)** options available are **Vertical Type, Vertical Type Mask,** and **Horizontal Type mask Tools**. Adobe defines the **Text Tool** as the word **Type Tool**. *Select the Horizontal Type Tool →Draw a square box→Type the text.*

2.8-1 Horizontal Type Tool Options

The following are the **Horizontal Type** options located just under **Menus** on top of the interface:

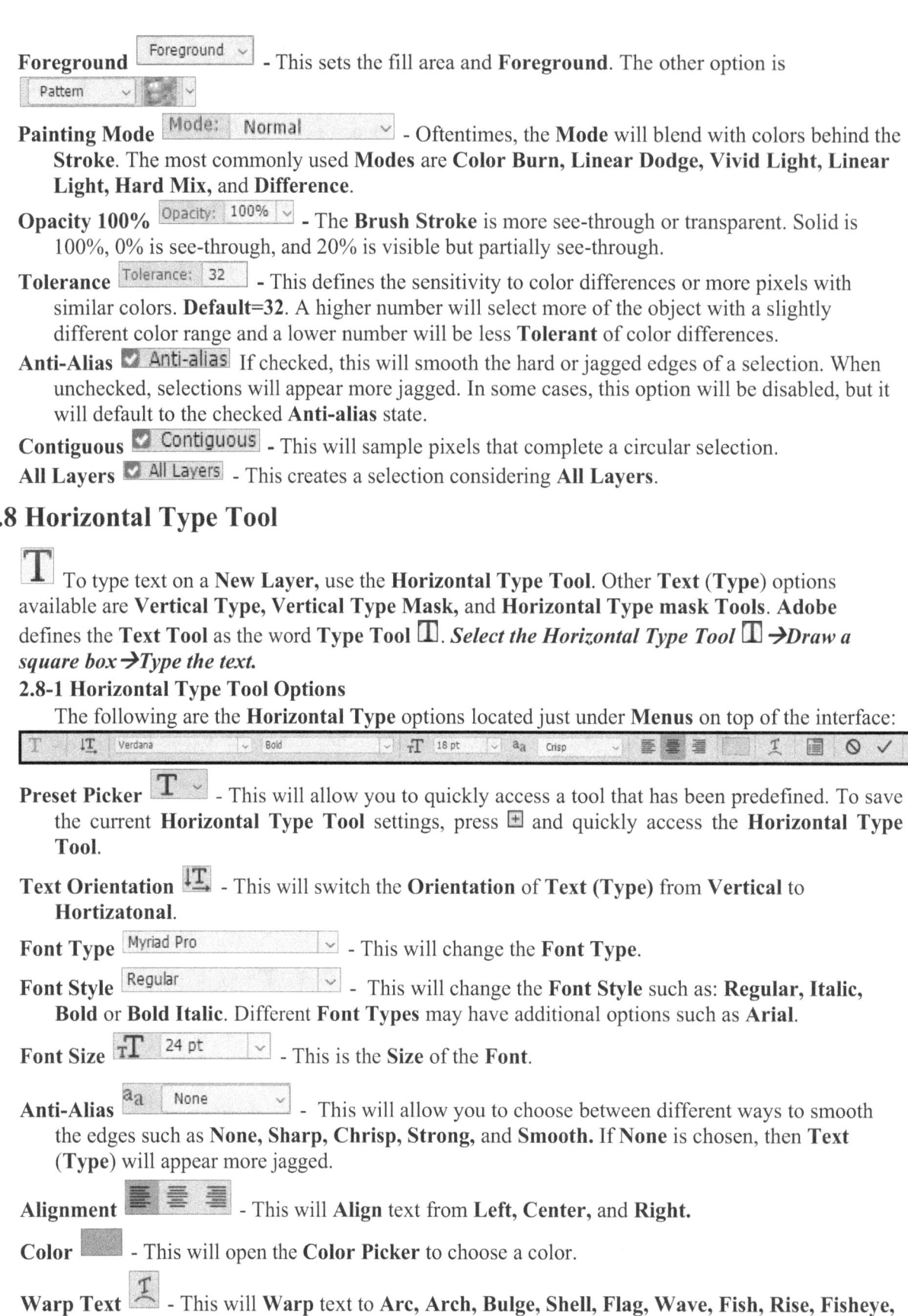

Preset Picker `T` - This will allow you to quickly access a tool that has been predefined. To save the current **Horizontal Type Tool** settings, press ⊞ and quickly access the **Horizontal Type Tool**.

Text Orientation `IT` - This will switch the **Orientation** of **Text (Type)** from **Vertical** to **Hortizatonal**.

Font Type `Myriad Pro` - This will change the **Font Type**.

Font Style `Regular` - This will change the **Font Style** such as: **Regular, Italic, Bold** or **Bold Italic**. Different **Font Types** may have additional options such as **Arial**.

Font Size `24 pt` - This is the **Size** of the **Font**.

Anti-Alias `None` - This will allow you to choose between different ways to smooth the edges such as **None, Sharp, Chrisp, Strong,** and **Smooth.** If **None** is chosen, then **Text (Type)** will appear more jagged.

Alignment - This will **Align** text from **Left, Center,** and **Right.**

Color - This will open the **Color Picker** to choose a color.

Warp Text - This will **Warp** text to **Arc, Arch, Bulge, Shell, Flag, Wave, Fish, Rise, Fisheye, Inflate, Squeeze,** or **Twist.**

Chapter 2 - In-Depth Drawing Tools

Toggle Panels - This will open or **Toggle** between the **Character** and **Paragraph Panels**.

3D Text - This will turn the **Text** (**Type**) into a **3D** look.

Practice Exercise 10 - Horizontal TypeTool

1. *File Menu→Open→Filename: C:\Data\Photoshopcc-2\Thomas Jefferson Memorial.jpg →* Open .

2. *Type a text title across the sky "Thomas Jefferson Memorial."*

2.9 Shape Tools

2.9-1 The following are the different **Shapes** available:

Rectangle Tool - This draws a rectangle and the **Shift** key will draw a square. Before you let go of the **left mouse,** hold the **Spacebar** to move the shape into place.

Rounded Rectangle Tool - This draws a rounded rectangle and the **Shift** key will draw a rounded square. Before you let go of the **left mouse,** hold the **Spacebar** to move the shape into place.

Ellipse Tool - This draws an **Ellipse** and the **Shift** key will draw a circle. Before you let go of the **left mouse,** hold the **Spacebar** to move the shape into place.

Polygon Tool - This draws a **Polygon** shape. Before you let go of the **left mouse** button, hold the **Spacebar** to move the shape into place.

Line Tool - This draws **Lines**. Hold the **Shift** key and it will draw 45-degree angles. Before you let go of the **left mouse,** hold the **Spacebar** to move the shape into place.

Custom Shape Tool - This draws different shapes. Hold the **Shift** key to scale the shape and hold the **Spacebar** to move the shape into place. *Custom Shape Tool →Options →Shapes dropdown* .

A **Custom Shape** can be formatted using the **Tool Bar Options**. Use the **Gear** to import additional shapes.

2.9-2 Shape Option

The following are the **Shape** options located just under **Menus** on top of the interface:

Preset Picker - This will allow you to quickly access a tool that has been predefined. To save the current **Shapes Tool** settings, press and quickly access the **Shapes Tool**.

Pick Tool Mode: Shape - **Shape Mode** will draw a vector object on a different layer. Using the **Move Tool**, you will be able to move an object.

Fill - This will set the **Fill** color of the object.

Stroke - This will define the **Stroke (Border)** and **Border** width.

Chapter 2 - In-Depth Drawing Tools

Stroke Type - This will define the line **Type** used.

Width/Height This will allow you to enter the physical **Height** and **Width** of a **Shape**.

Path Operations - These will affect the cross-section of overlapping objects in the following ways: Combine Shapes, Subtract Front Shape, Intersect Shape Areas, and Exclude Overlapping Shapes.

Align Options:

  Vertical Alignment - This will **Align** selected objects placed in different layers **Vertically**.

  Horizontal Alignment - This will **Align** selected objects placed in different layers **Horizontally**.

  Distribute - This will **Distribute** objects placed in different layers **Vertically** or **Horizontally**.

  Distribute Spacing - This will evenly space the objects placed on different layers **Vertically** or **Horizontally**.

Path Arrangement - This will arrange overlapping objects to Bring Shape To Front, Bring Shape Forward, Send Shape Backward, and Send Shape to Back.

Path Options - This will adjust the **Path** of an object for **Thickness, Color, Unconstrained, Square, Fixed Size, Proportional,** and **From Center.**

Radius - This will define the **Radius** for corners.

Align Edges - This will **Align** a vector **Shape** with other **Shapes** on different layers based on the defined **Pixel Grid**. It seems, however, to have little effect on **Aligning Shape Edges**.

2.9-3 Path Option

The following are the **Path** options located just under **Menus** on top of the interface:

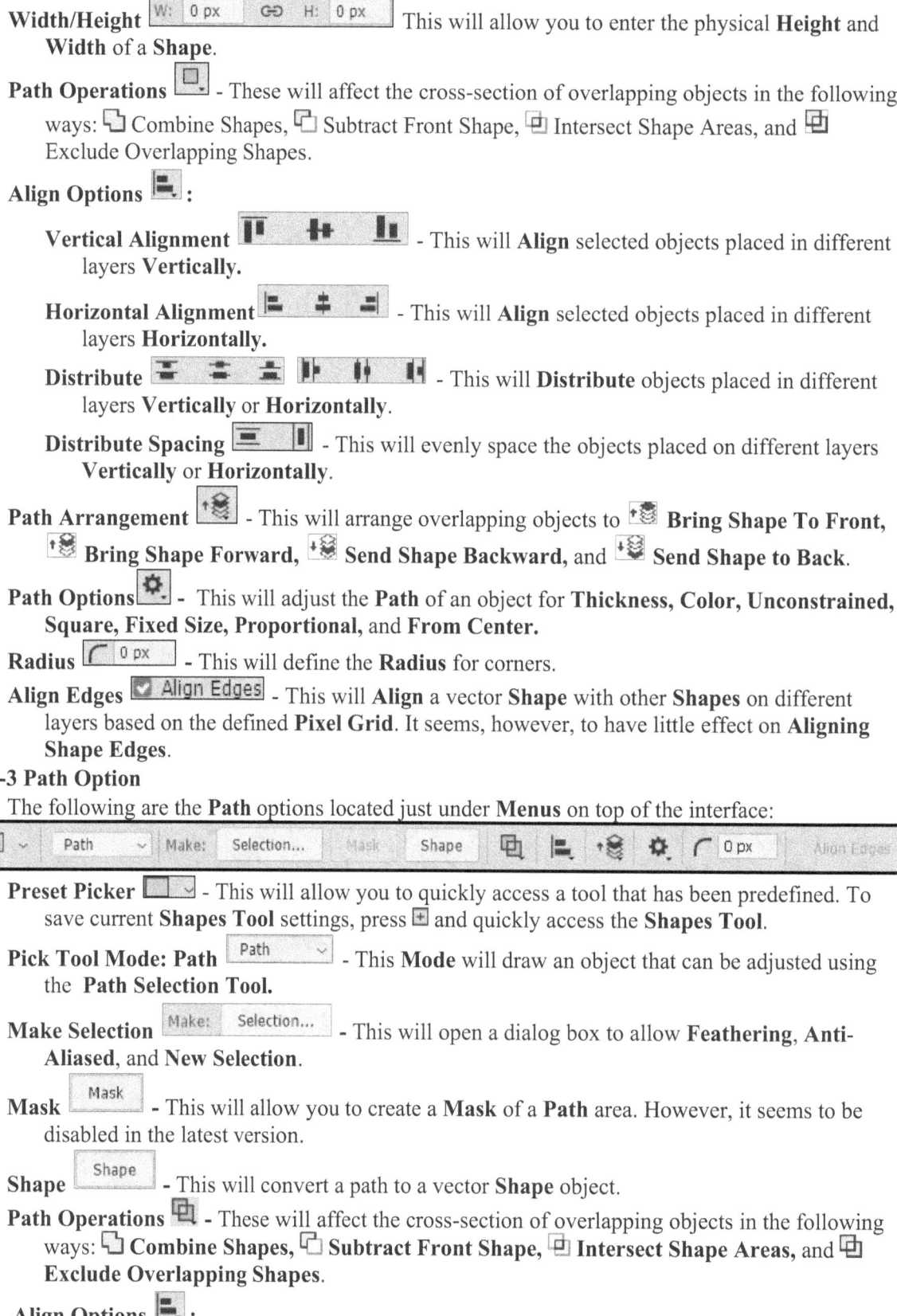

Preset Picker - This will allow you to quickly access a tool that has been predefined. To save current **Shapes Tool** settings, press and quickly access the **Shapes Tool**.

Pick Tool Mode: Path - This **Mode** will draw an object that can be adjusted using the **Path Selection Tool.**

Make Selection - This will open a dialog box to allow **Feathering, Anti-Aliased,** and **New Selection**.

Mask - This will allow you to create a **Mask** of a **Path** area. However, it seems to be disabled in the latest version.

Shape - This will convert a path to a vector **Shape** object.

Path Operations - These will affect the cross-section of overlapping objects in the following ways: **Combine Shapes, Subtract Front Shape, Intersect Shape Areas,** and **Exclude Overlapping Shapes**.

Align Options:

Chapter 2 - In-Depth Drawing Tools

Vertical Alignment - This will **Align** selected objects placed in different layers **Vertically.**

Horizontal Alignment - This will **Align** selected objects placed in different layers **Horizontally.**

Distribute - This will **Distribute** objects placed in different layers **Vertically** or **Horizontally.**

Distribute Spacing - This will evenly space objects placed on different layers **Vertically** or **Horizontally**.

Path Arrangement - This will arrange overlapping objects to **Bring Shape To Front, Bring Shape Forward, Send Shape Backward,** and **Send Sgape to Back.**

Path Options - This will adjust a **Path** of an object for **Thickness, Color, Unconstrained, Square, Fixed Size, Proportional,** and **From Center.**

Radius - This will define the **Radius** for corners.

Align Edges - This will **Align** a vector **Shape** with other **Shapes** on different layers based on the defined **Pixel Grid**. It seems, however, to have little effect on **Aligning** the **Shape Edges**.

2.9-4 Pixels Options

The following are the **Pixels** options located just under **Menus** on top of the interface:

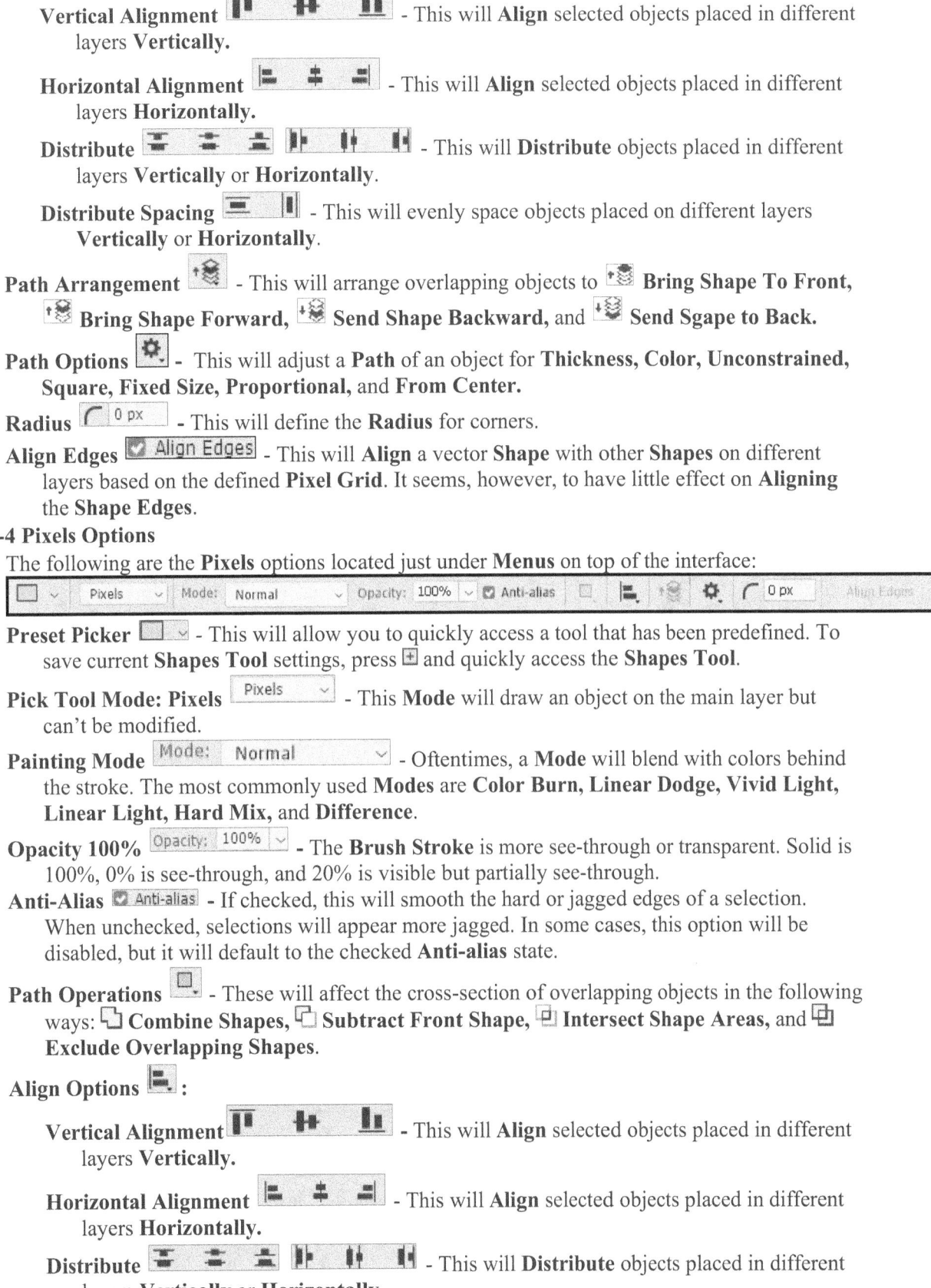

Preset Picker - This will allow you to quickly access a tool that has been predefined. To save current **Shapes Tool** settings, press and quickly access the **Shapes Tool**.

Pick Tool Mode: Pixels - This **Mode** will draw an object on the main layer but can't be modified.

Painting Mode - Oftentimes, a **Mode** will blend with colors behind the stroke. The most commonly used **Modes** are **Color Burn, Linear Dodge, Vivid Light, Linear Light, Hard Mix,** and **Difference**.

Opacity 100% - The **Brush Stroke** is more see-through or transparent. Solid is 100%, 0% is see-through, and 20% is visible but partially see-through.

Anti-Alias - If checked, this will smooth the hard or jagged edges of a selection. When unchecked, selections will appear more jagged. In some cases, this option will be disabled, but it will default to the checked **Anti-alias** state.

Path Operations - These will affect the cross-section of overlapping objects in the following ways: **Combine Shapes, Subtract Front Shape, Intersect Shape Areas,** and **Exclude Overlapping Shapes.**

Align Options :

Vertical Alignment - This will **Align** selected objects placed in different layers **Vertically.**

Horizontal Alignment - This will **Align** selected objects placed in different layers **Horizontally.**

Distribute - This will **Distribute** objects placed in different layers **Vertically** or **Horizontally.**

Chapter 2 - In-Depth Drawing Tools

Distribute Spacing - This will evenly space objects placed on different layers **Vertically** or **Horizontally**.

Path Arrangement - This will arrange overlapping objects to **Bring Shape To Front**, **Bring Shape Forward**, **Send Shape Backward**, and **Send Sgape to Back**.

Path Options - This will adjust the **Path** of an object for **Thickness, Color, Unconstrained, Square, Fixed Size, Proportional,** and **From Center**.

Radius - This will define the **Radius** for corners.

Align Edges - This will **Align** a vector **Shape** with other **Shapes** on different layers based on the defined **Pixel Grid**. This seems, however, to have little effect on **Aligning Shape Edges**.

Practice Exercise 11 - Align And Distribute

1. *File Menu→New→Print Tab→Print Presets→Letter (8.5 x 11 in @ 300 ppi→* Create.
2. *Draw 3 shapes: Rectangular Tool→Draw 3 rectangles.*
3. *Select all 3 rectangle Layers using the* Ctrl *and* Shift *keys.*
4. *Use the Align and Distribute features.*

Practice Exercise 12 - Shapes

File Menu →New→ Print Tab→Print Presets→Letter (8.5 x 11 in @ 300 ppi→ Create.

Choose Custom Shape Tool→Shapes Dropdown → *Choose a shape→Draw the shapes using the* Spacebar *to move the shape,* Shift *key to draw it proportional, and* Alt *key to draw it from the center.*

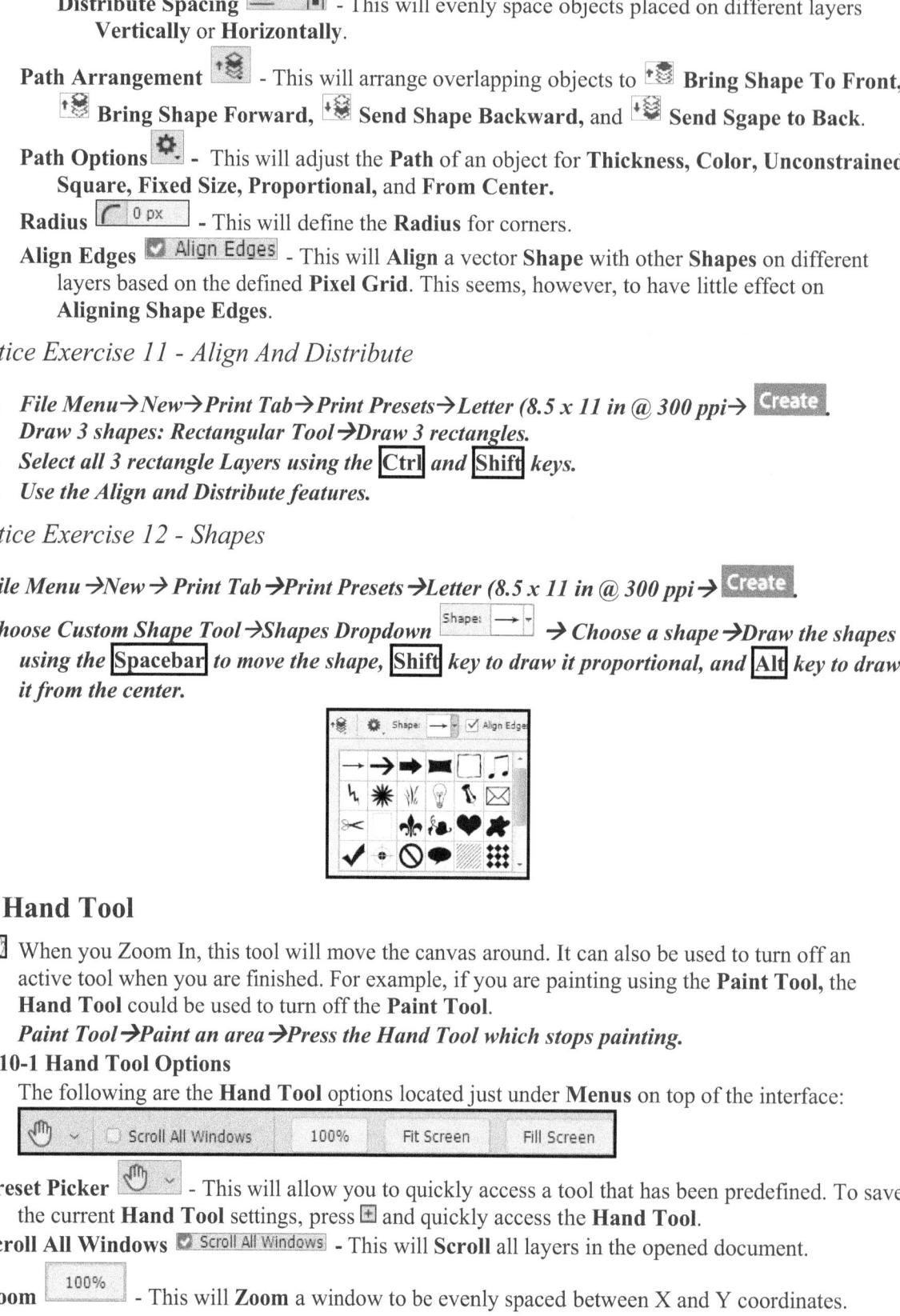

2.10 Hand Tool

When you Zoom In, this tool will move the canvas around. It can also be used to turn off an active tool when you are finished. For example, if you are painting using the **Paint Tool**, the **Hand Tool** could be used to turn off the **Paint Tool**.

Paint Tool→Paint an area→Press the Hand Tool which stops painting.

2.10-1 Hand Tool Options

The following are the **Hand Tool** options located just under **Menus** on top of the interface:

Preset Picker - This will allow you to quickly access a tool that has been predefined. To save the current **Hand Tool** settings, press ⊞ and quickly access the **Hand Tool**.

Scroll All Windows - This will **Scroll** all layers in the opened document.

Zoom - This will **Zoom** a window to be evenly spaced between X and Y coordinates.

Chapter 2 - In-Depth Drawing Tools

Fit Screen 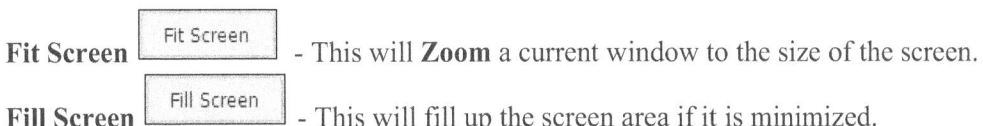 - This will **Zoom** a current window to the size of the screen.

Fill Screen - This will fill up the screen area if it is minimized.

Practice Exercise 13 - Tools

1. *File Menu→Open→C:\Data\PhotoshopCC-2\Maestro.jpg→* Open .

2. *Zoom in→Use the Hand Tool to move the canvas. Practice the above tools covered in this chapter.*

Section 2: Optional Tools

The following are optional concepts or features that are not commonly used. They are advanced or alternate techniques compared to the ones previously mentioned in sections of this chapter.

Section Table Of Contents:

    2.11 Color Replacement Tool   2.20 Note Tool
    2.12 Mixer Brush Tool   2.21 Count Tool
    2.13 Background Eraser Tool   2.22 Magic Eraser Tool
    2.14 Color Sampler Tool   2.23 Slice Tool
    2.15 Art History Brush Tool   2.24 Slice Select Tool
    2.16 Gradient Tool   2.25 Brush Defaults
    2.17 Pattern Stamp Tool   2.26 Add New Brushes
    2.18 Create Custom Patterns   2.27 Create New Brushes
    2.19 Ruler Tool

2.11 Color Replacement Tool

This mixes a sampled color with the existing color. Use the options to clean a brush when you're ready to color a new area. Use the **Alt** (**Mac CS6:** *Use the* **option** *key)* to sample a good area and draw on a new area to **Replace** a **Color**.

2.11-1 Color Replacement Tool Options

The following are the **Color Replacement Tool** options located just under **Menus** on top of the interface:

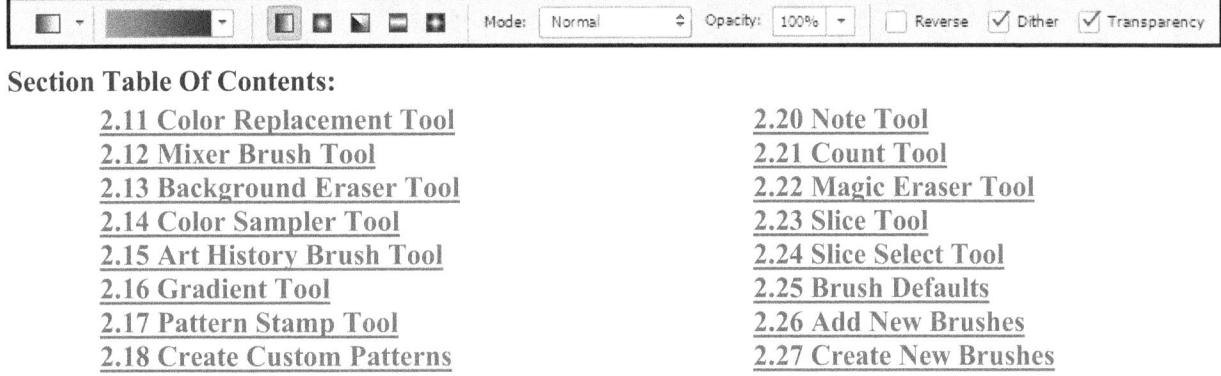

Preset Picker - This will allow you to quickly access a tool that has been predefined. To save the current **Color Replacement Tool** settings, press ⊞ and quickly access the **Color Replacement Tool**.

Color Replacement Characteristics:

Brush Size: →*Brush Preset Picker dropdown* →

Brush Hardness: →*Brush Preset Picker dropdown* →

Brushes: →*Brush Preset Picker dropdown* →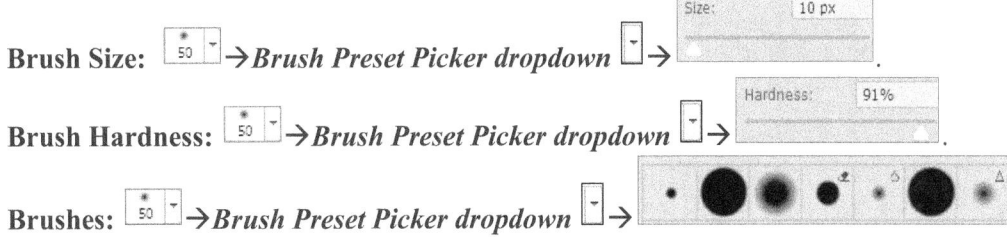

Page 21

Color Mode — The default **Mode** is **Color**. **Hue** mode will not change saturation or brightness, but it will only change basic colors. **Saturation** is used to change the intensity of color or eliminate them. **Luminosity** affects the brightness of the original color.

Sampling: Continuous — This is the default setting that continues looking for new colors to replace as you drag using this tool.

Sampling: Once — This will only **Sample** the initial click and is used for replacing a large area of color.

Sampling: Background Swatch — This will **Sample** any color that matches a **Background** color.

Replacement Color — This controls where a tool can look for colors to replace. **Contiguous** (default setting) means it can only change pixels that are in the same area where the cursor is touching. **Discontiguous** is the opposite effect. **Find Edges** is similar to **Contiguous** but it's better at detecting **Edges**.

Tolerance — This defines sensitivity to color differences or more pixels with similar colors. **Default=32**. The higher number will select more of an object with a slightly different color range, and a lower number will be less **Tolerant** of color differences.

Anti-Alias If checked, this will smooth hard or jagged edges of a selection. When unchecked, selections will appear more jagged. In some cases, this option will be disabled but it will default to the checked **Anti-alias** state.

Brush Angle — This will set an **Angle** when you begin to draw. It is not noticeable in normal situations, however.

Pressure For Size — Always use **Pressure For Size**. When turned off, **Brush Preset** controls **Pressure**. This works best with a tablet pen rather than a mouse.

Practice Exercise 14 - Color Replacement

File Menu→Open→C:\Data\PhotoshopCC-2\Balloons.jpg→ Open .

Select Color Replacement Tool → Alt Click the green Balloon→Paint the green color on the yellow balloon. **Mac CS6:** *Use the* option *key to sample the color.*

2.12 Mixer Brush Tool

If you brush crossing over several colors, the colors will mix. This could be used to blur between color edges.

2.12-1 Mixer Brush Tool Options

The following are the **Mixer Brush Tool** options located just under **Menus** on top of the interface:

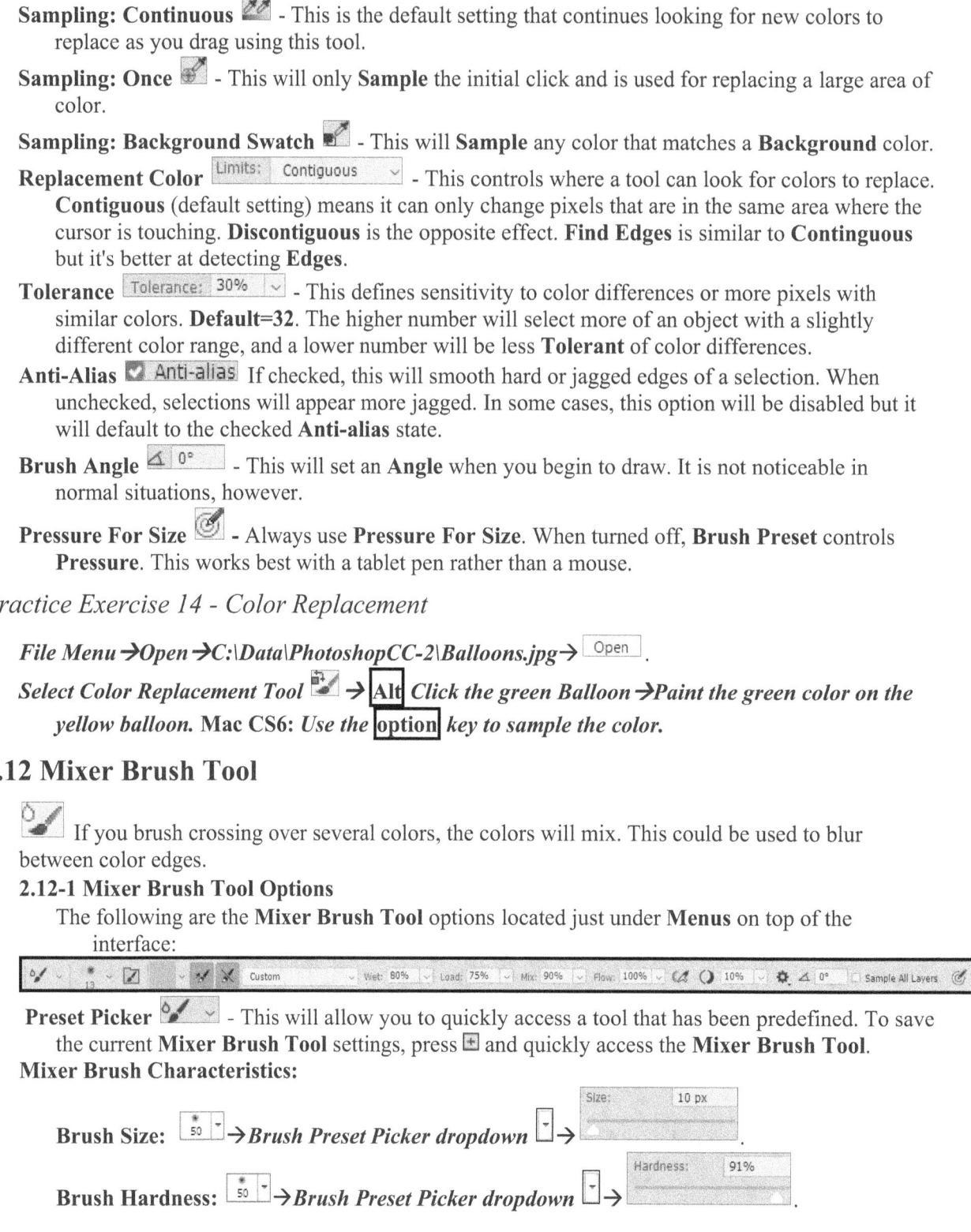

Preset Picker — This will allow you to quickly access a tool that has been predefined. To save the current **Mixer Brush Tool** settings, press ⊞ and quickly access the **Mixer Brush Tool**.

Mixer Brush Characteristics:

Brush Size: →*Brush Preset Picker dropdown* →.

Brush Hardness: →*Brush Preset Picker dropdown* →.

Brushes: [50] → *Brush Preset Picker dropdown* → .

Brush Settings Panel - This will toggle the **Brush Settings Panel**.

Color - This changes the primary color of the **Mixer Brush Tool.**

Load Brush - This will **Load** the **Brush** after each stroke with a currently defined color.

Clean Brush - This will **Clear** the **Brush** color settings after each stroke.

Mixer Brush [Custom] - This will adjust the **Wet** [Wet: 80%] which lays wet paint on a canvas, **Load** [Load: 75%] will place more paint on the **Brush**, and **Mix** [Mix: 90%] will adjust the mixing ratio when using the stroke:

Custom - This will adjust the Wet, Load, and Mix parameters as desired.
Dry - This will define **Wet: 0% Load: 50% Mix:**
Dry, Light Load - This will define **Wet: 0% Load: 5% Mix:**
Dry, Heavy Load - This will define **Wet: 0% Load: 100% Mix:**
Moist - This will define **Wet: 10% Load: 5% Mix: 50%**
Moist, Light Mix - This will define **Wet: 10% Load: 5% Mix: 0%**
Moist, Heavy Mix - This will define **Wet: 10% Load: 5% Mix: 100%**
Wet - This will define **Wet: 50% Load: 50% Mix: 50%**
Wet, Light Mix - This will define **Wet: 50% Load: 50% Mix: 0%**
Wet, Heavy Mix - This will define **Wet: 50% Load: 50% Mix: 100%**
Very Wet - This will define **Wet: 100% Load: 50% Mix: 50%**
Very Wet, Light Mix - This will define **Wet: 100% Load: 50% Mix: 0%**
Very Wet, Heavy Mix - This will define **Wet: 100% Load: 50% Mix: 100%**

Flow [Flow: 100%] - This is a percentage that sets the rate of color applied or the amount of ink that is applied to a tool.

Airbrush - This simulates painting with an **Airbrush**.

Smoothing [10%] - This will **Smooth** the **Stroke** (border) edges. A higher value will make a **Stroke Smoother** as you draw.

Brush Smoothing Options - This will adjust **Smoothing** options such as **Pulled String Mode, Stroke Catch-up, Catch-up on Stroke End,** and **Adjust for Zoom.**

Brush Angle [0°] - This will set an **Angle** when you begin to draw. This is not noticeable in normal situations.

Sample All Layers [Sample All Layers] - This will identify the applied web paint from **All Layers**.

Pressure For Size - Always use **Pressure For Size**. When turned off, **Brush Preset** controls **Pressure**. This works best with a tablet pen rather than a mouse.

Practice Exercise 15 - Mixer Brush

File Menu→Open→C:\Data\PhotoshopCC-2\Balloons.jpg→ [Open].
Select the Mixer Brush Tool→Draw the lines between the balloons.

2.13 Background Eraser Tool

This erases one layer below but doesn't **Erase** critical top layer pixels.

2.13-1 Background Eraser Tool Options

Chapter 2 - In-Depth Drawing Tools

The following are the **Background Eraser Tool** options located just under **Menus** on top of the interface:

Preset Picker - This will allow you to quickly access a tool that has been predefined. To save the current **Background Eraser Tool** settings, press ⊞ and quickly access the **Background Eraser Tool**.

Background Eraser Characteristics:

Brush Size: → *Brush Preset Picker dropdown* → .

Brush Hardness: → *Brush Preset Picker dropdown* → .

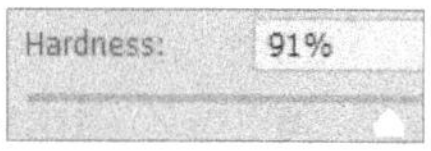

Brushes: → *Brush Preset Picker dropdown* → .

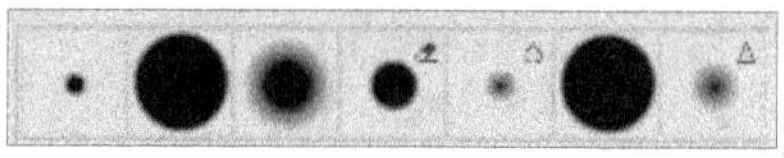

Sampling: Continuous - This is the default setting that continues searching for new colors to replace as you drag using this tool.

Sampling: Once - This will only **Sample** an initial click and is used for replacing a large area of color.

Sampling: Background Swatch - This will be any color that matches a **Background** color.

Limits - This puts **Limits** on the replaced color based on **Contiguous** area, **Discontiguous** area, or **Edges**.

Tolerance - This defines sensitivity to color differences or more pixels with similar colors. **Default=32**. The higher number will select more of an object with a slightly different color range, and a lower number is less **Tolerant** of color differences.

Brush Angle - This will set an **Angle** as you begin to draw. It is not noticeable in normal situations, however.

Protect Foreground Color - This will prevent the **Foreground** swatch color from being erased.

Pressure For Size - Always use **Pressure For Size**. When turned off, **Brush Preset** controls **Pressure**. This works best with a tablet pen rather than a mouse.

Practice Exercise 16 - Background Eraser

Erase the **Background** of the **Baby Bracelet**.
1. *File Menu → Open → C:\Data\PhotoshopCC-2\Backdrop.jpg →* Open
2. *File Menu → Open → C:\Data\PhotoshopCC-2\BabyBracelet.jpg →* Open .
3. *Window Menu → Arrange → ▥ Tile All Vertically.*
4. *Move Tool → Move the BabyBracelet to the Backdrop picture.*
5. *Select the Background Eraser Tool → Set the options to the following settings:*

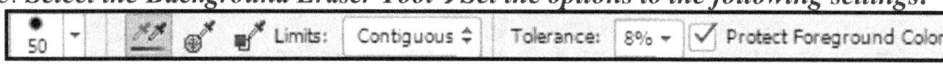

6. *Gently click on the edges of the bracelet.*

Student Project A - Replacing Background

1. *File Menu → Open → C:\Data\PhotoshopCC-2\Harbor.jpg →* Open .
2. *File Menu → Open → C:\Data\PhotoshopCC-2\Countryside.jpg →* Open .

Chapter 2 - In-Depth Drawing Tools

3. *Move Tool→Drag Countryside to Harbor→Rename Countryside Layer Name: Good Sky→Close the file Countryside.jpg.*
4. *Create a new Layer of Harbor: In the Layers Panel, drag the background layer to create a ⌸ New Layer.*
5. *Rearrange the layers as follows:*

6. *Use the Polygon Selection Tool to do a rough delete of the sky around the boat and land of the Harbor Sky→Press Delete key.* See example.

7. *Select→Deselect.*
8. *Background Erase Tool→Delete the remaining Harbor sky.*
   Change Brush Tool (Diameter: 100, Hardness: 50.
   Use the center point as the sample point→Click, Click.

2.14 Color Sampler Tool

This allows you to **Sample** several areas and compare the **RGB** or **CMYK** differences. ***Window Menu→Info Panel.*** It doesn't generate an average of **Color Samples**, but you can see the **RGB** and **CMYK** colors chosen in the **Info Panel**. Use the **Shift** key to move a **Sample** to a new position or simply hold your mouse over the **Sample** until the cursor changes and then move the **Sample**. Also, hold the **Alt** key over a **Sample** point to remove it. An alternate technique is to use the **Eye Dropper Tool** and hold the **Shift** key to switch to the **Color Sampler Tool**.

2.14-1 Color Sampler Tool Options

The following are the **Color Sampler Tool** options located just under **Menus** on top of the interface:

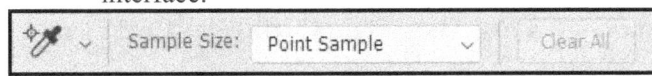

Preset Picker - This will allow you to quickly access a tool that has been predefined. To save the current **Color Sampler Tool** settings, press ⊞ and quickly access the **Color Sampler Tool**.

Sample Size - Instead of choosing the single pixel **Point Sample**, you can choose multiple pixel sample areas such as **3 by 3 Average, 5 by 5 Average**, etc. This can be used when color includes varying shades of colors.

Clear All - This will **Clear All Color Samples** in order to start over.

Practice Exercise 17 - Color Sampler Tool

Chapter 2 - In-Depth Drawing Tools

Continue from the previous practice exercise:
Select Color Sampler Tool→Sample the water: Click, Click, Click→Review the mixed color in the color picker. Choose Clear in the Options to start over.

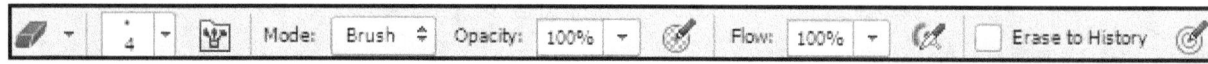

2.15 Art History Brush Tool

This allows you to paint over an image with a stylized version of a previously specified state.
Select area →Art History Brush Tool→Paint over the area.

2.15-1 Art History Brush Tool Options

The following are the **Art History Brush Tool** options located just under **Menus** on top of the interface:

Preset Picker - This will allow you to quickly access a tool that has been predefined. To save the current **Art History Brush Tool** settings, press ⊞ and quickly access the **Art History Brush Tool**.

History Brush Characteristics:

Brush Size: →*Brush Preset Picker dropdown* →.

Brush Hardness: →*Brush Preset Picker dropdown* →.

Brushes: →*Brush Preset Picker dropdown* →.

Brush Settings Panel or - This will toggle the **Brush Settings Panel**.

Painting Mode - Oftentimes, the **Mode** will blend with colors behind a stroke. The most commonly used **Modes** are **Color Burn, Linear Dodge, Vivid Light, Linear Light, Hard Mix,** and **Difference**.

Opacity 100% - The **Brush Stroke** is more see-through or transparent. Solid is 100%, 0% is see-through, and 20% is visible but partially see-through.

Pressure for Opacity - The **Opacity** will change depending on the amount of **Pressure** applied using a tablet pen (not a mouse). When turned off, **Brush Preset** controls **Pressure**.

Style - This will adjust **Art History** results based on **Tight Short, Tight Medium, Tight Long, Loose Medium, Loose Long, Dab, Tight Curl, Tight Curl Long, Loose Curl,** and **Loose Curl Long**. Each style will produce a different result.

Area - This is the diameter of the painting **Area**.

Tolerance - This defines sensitivity to color differences or more pixels with similar colors. **Default=0%**. The lower the number, more distortion will be applied and the higher the number less distortion will be applied.

Brush Angle - This will set an **Angle** as you begin to draw. It is not noticeable in normal situations.

Pressure For Size - Always use **Pressure For Size**. When turned off, **Brush Preset** controls **Pressure**. This works best with a tablet pen rather than a mouse.

Chapter 2 - In-Depth Drawing Tools

Practice Exercise 18 - Art History Brush

File Menu →Open →C:\Data\PhotoshopCC-2\Landscape.jpg → Open .
Art History Brush Tool →*Paint the photo →Change the style to Loose Medium →Paint the photo.*

2.16 Gradient Tool

The **Gradient Tool** is located under the **Paint Bucket Tool.** One of the major characteristics is the **Stop Points** that define where **Gradient Stops** and begins to transition to the next color. Three **Stop Points** are available by default, but more can be added if needed.

Gradient Dialog Box - Click on the **Gradient Dialog Box** which is located on the left side of all options for opening a dialog box. 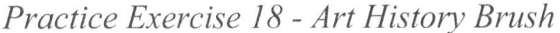 (Double-click if necessary).

Modify Stop Color - Double-click on the square box (see below) to change the **Gradient Color.**

Move Stop Point - Drag the stop box to the left or right to change the position of a **Gradient** transition.

Add New Stop Color - Click below the **Gradient Bar** between the stop boxes.

2.16-1 Gradient Tool Options

The following are the **Gradient Tool** options located just under **Menus** on top of the interface:

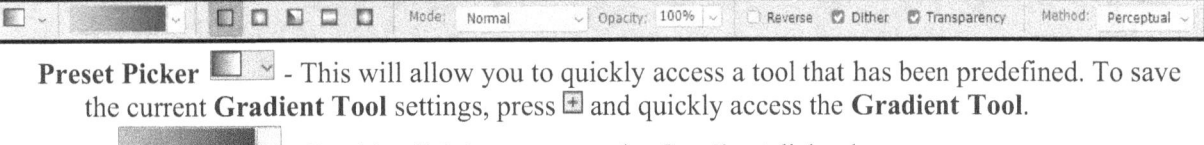

Preset Picker - This will allow you to quickly access a tool that has been predefined. To save the current **Gradient Tool** settings, press ⊞ and quickly access the **Gradient Tool**.

Color - Double-click here to open the **Gradient** dialog box.

Linear Gradient - This will create a progressive transition between two or more colors along a straight line.

Radial Gradient - This creates an image consisting of a progressive transition between two or more colors starting from an original point.

Angle Gradient - This will create a progressive transition between two or more colors at an **Angle**.

Reflected Gradient - This will create a mirror image of a **Linear Gradient** on either side of a starting point.

Diamond Gradient - This will create a **Diamond** pattern that shades from the middle to the outer corners.

Painting Mode - Oftentimes, a **Mode** will blend with the colors behind the stroke. The most commonly used **Modes** are **Color Burn, Linear Dodge, Vivid Light, Linear Light, Hard Mix,** and **Difference**.

Opacity 100% - The **Brush Stroke** is more see-through or transparent. Solid is 100%, 0% is see-through, and 20% is visible but partially see-through.

Reverse - This will reverse the displayed **Gradient**.

Dither - This will create a smoother bend on rounded edges.

Transparency - This will allow the fill area to gradually blend into an ending color.

Chapter 2 - In-Depth Drawing Tools

Method [Method: Perceptual] - This will adjust **Gradient** colors based on **Perceptual**, **Linear**, and **Classic** methods.

Practice Exercise 19 - Gradient Tool

1. *File Menu→New→ Print Tab→Print Presets→Letter (8.5 x 11 in @ 300 ppi→* [Create].
2. *Select the Gradient Tool→Specify the Gradient style* [____] *in the Gradient options.*
3. *Draw a line several times across the drawing area.*
   Tip: The start of the line will be the beginning of a primary color.
   The end of the line will be the last color in the gradient.

Practice Exercise 20 - Gradient Color

1. *Rectangular Marque Tool* [] *→Draw a box.*
2. *Click on the Gradient Tool→Double-click on the Gradient color box* [____] *→Modify the stop colors →* [____] *→* [OK].
3. *Draw a line across the selected box.* **Tip**: The start of the line will be the beginning of a primary color. The end of the line will be the last color in the gradient.

2.17 Pattern Stamp Tool

This tool allows you to create unique **Patterns** from existing areas (**Stamped**).

Create Pattern: *Rectangular Marquee Tool →Select area→Edit Menu →Define Pattern.*
Pattern Stamp Tool →Choose Pattern in the Options [] *→ Paint Pattern.*

2.17-1 Pattern Stamp Tool Options

The following are the **Pattern Stamp Tool** options located just under **Menus** on top of the interface:

Preset Picker [] - This will allow you to quickly access a tool that has been predefined. To save the current **Pattern Stamp Tool** settings, press [+] and quickly access the **Pattern Stamp Tool**.

Pattern Stamp Preset picker - [7] This will change the **Pattern Size** and hardness.

Use the Pattern Stamp Preset Picker drop-down [7] *→Pattern Stamp Preset Picker Menu* [] *to choose additional brushes.*

Pattern Stamp Brush Characteristics:

Brush Size: [50] *→Brush Preset Picker dropdown* [] *→* [Size: 10 px].

Brush Hardness: [50] *→Brush Preset Picker dropdown* [] *→* [Hardness: 91%].

Brushes: [50] *→Brush Preset Picker dropdown* [] *→* [].

Brush Settings Panel [] - This will toggle the **Brush Settings Panel.**

Chapter 2 - In-Depth Drawing Tools

Mode Normal `Mode: Normal` - Oftentimes, a **Mode** will blend with colors behind a brush stroke. **Tip:** Draw using **Hard light** vs. **Vivid Light** to see the differences.

Opacity `Opacity: 100%` - A brush stroke is more see-through or transparent. **Usually 100%.**

Pressure for Opacity - The **Opacity** will change depending on the amount of **Pressure** applied using a tablet pen (**not a mouse**). When turned off, the brush preset controls **Pressure**.

Flow `Flow: 100%` - This is a percentage that sets the rate of color applied or the amount of ink that is applied to the tool.

Airbrush - This simulates painting with an **Airbrush** machine.

Brush Angle `0°` - This will set an **Angle** when you begin to draw. This is not noticeable in normal situations.

Pattern - This will allow you to choose the desired **Pattern**.

Aligned `☑ Aligned` - This will **Align** each stroke side by side even if you start the second stroke in a different position. If left unchecked, it will be random strokes.

Impressionist - This could be used for facial patterns and even gives a facial pigment effect.
`☐ Impressionist` - This can appear choppy when unchecked. Also, in older versions, however, the icon was .
`☑ Impressionist` - When checked, it blends and seems smoother. In older versions, the icon was .

Pressure For Size - Always use **Pressure For Size**. When turned off, brush preset controls **Pressure**. This works best with a tablet pen rather than a mouse.

Practice Exercise 21 - Aligned

1. *File Menu→New→ Print Tab→Print Presets→Letter (8.5 x 11 in @ 300 ppi→* `Create`.
2. *Pattern Stamp Tool→Choose a pattern* .
3. *Change the brush size to 200* `200`.
4. *Draw the pattern→ Turn the Align option on* `☑ Aligned` *→Turn Impressionist off* `☐ Impressionist` *→Draw a pattern and fill up the top part of the screen.*
5. *Turn the Align option off* `☐ Aligned` *→Draw a pattern to view the Stamp Tool.*

2.18 Create Custom Patterns

This defines a new **Pattern** from a file or selected area.
Open a File→Select a Pattern on the image→ Edit Menu→Define Pattern→Name →Pattern Stamp Tool→Choose the pattern→Draw the pattern on a new sheet.

Practice Exercise 22 - Create Pattern

1. *File Menu→Open →C:\Data\PhotoshopCC-2\BabyBracelet.jpg→* `Open`.
2. *Crop Tool→Draw a rectangle around one of the beads→ click the ✓ to finish the cropping or hit the* `Enter` *key.*
3. *Edit Menu → Define Pattern→Pattern Name: Bead→* `OK`.

Chapter 2 - In-Depth Drawing Tools

4. *File Menu→New→ Print Tab→Print Presets→Letter (8.5 x 11 in @ 300 ppi→* Create.
5. *Pattern Stamp Tool→Choose the defined pattern* .
6. *Change the brush size to 200* .
7. *Paint the new pattern.*

Practice Exercise 23 - Impressionist

1. *File Menu→Open→C:\Data\PhotoshopCC-2\Executive.jpg→* Open.
2. *Rectangle Marquee Tool→Draw a rectangle to capture a pattern of the executive's face/skin.*
3. *Edit Menu→Define Pattern→ Pattern Name: Face→* OK.
4. *Pattern Stamp Tool→Choose the defined pattern* .
5. *Change the brush size to 200* .
6. *Select Menu→Deselect.*
7. *Select* ☑ Impressionist *→Draw the Impression.*

Test It: Try it out with **Impressionist** checked and unchecked.

2.19 Ruler Tool

This will measure distances. *Select the Ruler Tool→Click Drag the left mouse button to measure the distance→Let go of the mouse.*

2.19-1 Ruler Tool Options
The following are the **Ruler Tool** options located just under **Menus** on top of the interface:

Preset Picker - This will allow you to quickly access a tool that has been predefined. To save the current **Ruler Tool** settings, press ⊞ and quickly access the **Ruler Tool**.

Position - This will display results of a defined **Ruler** distance. **Tip**: View the **Position** in the **Info Panel**: *Window→Info.*

Use Measurement Scale - This will use the defined **Measurement Scale**:
- When unchecked, it will display units with no decimal places:
- When checked, it will display units with decimal places:

Straighten Layer - This will adjust a layer based on the angle of the line.
Test It: *Select a layer→Draw the ruler line at an angle→Strengthen Layer.*

Clear - This will **Clear** previously defined settings.

2.20 Note Tool

This adds a **Note** that could be used to identify the origin of an image. Open the **Notes Panel** to enter the **Note** text: *Window Menu→Notes.* **Tip**: These icons do not print when an image is printed.

2.20-1 Note Tool Options
The following are the **Note Tool** options located just under **Menus** on top of the interface:

Chapter 2 - In-Depth Drawing Tools

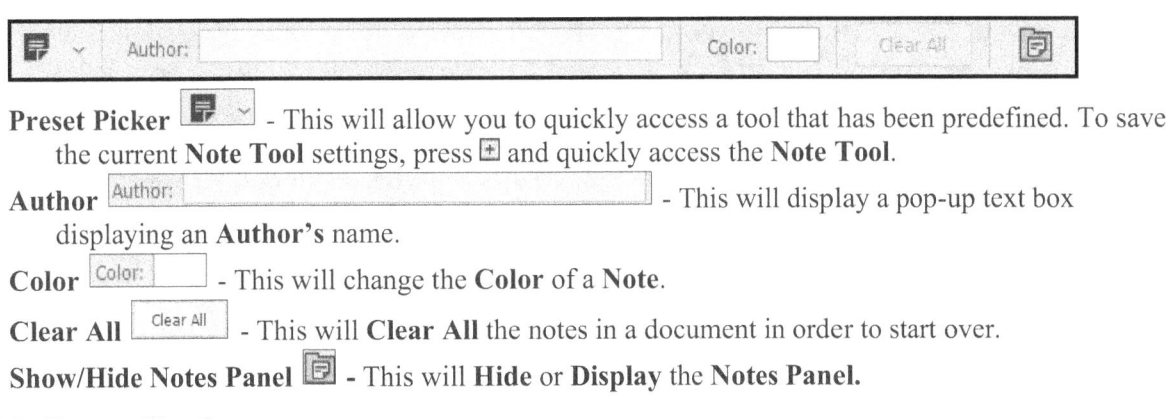

Preset Picker - This will allow you to quickly access a tool that has been predefined. To save the current **Note Tool** settings, press ⊞ and quickly access the **Note Tool**.

Author - This will display a pop-up text box displaying an **Author's** name.

Color - This will change the **Color** of a **Note**.

Clear All - This will **Clear All** the notes in a document in order to start over.

Show/Hide Notes Panel - This will **Hide** or **Display** the **Notes Panel.**

2.21 Count Tool

This places numbers on an image from 1, 2, 3, 4, 5, 6, etc.

2.21-1 Count Tool Options

The following are the **Count Tool** options located just under **Menus** on top of the interface:

Preset Picker - This will allow you to quickly access a tool that has been predefined. To save the current **Count Tool** settings, press ⊞ and quickly access **Count Tool**.

Count - This will specify the number to **Count**.

Count Group - This will list multiple **Groups** of **Counting**.

Visibility - This causes numbers to disappear.

New Count Group - This will start a new series of **Counting** numbers.

Delete Group - This will **Delete** a **Group** of numbers.

Clear - This will **Clear** all numbers to start over.

Group Color - This will allow you to identify each **Group** defined by size.

Marker Size - This will define the **Size** of the number.

Label Size - This will define the **Size** of the **Label.**

2.22 Magic Eraser Tool

This **Erases** pixels with similar color shades.

2.22-1 Magic Eraser Tool Options

The following are the **Magic Eraser Tool** options located just under **Menus** on top of the interface:

Preset Picker - This will allow you to quickly access a tool that has been predefined. To save the current **Magic Eraser Tool** settings, press ⊞ and quickly access the **Magic Eraser Tool**.

Tolerance - This defines sensitivity to color differences or more pixels with similar colors. **Default=32**. The higher number will select more of an object with a slightly different color range, and a lower number will be less **Tolerant** of color differences.

Chapter 2 - In-Depth Drawing Tools

Anti-Alias - If checked, this will smooth the hard or jagged edges of a selection. When unchecked, selections will appear more jagged. In some cases, this option will be disabled, but it will default to the checked **Anti-alias** state.

Contiguous - This will sample pixels that complete a circular selection.

Sample All Layers - This will identify applied paint from **All Layers**.

Opacity - The **Brush Stroke** is more see-through or transparent. Solid is 100%, 0% is see-through, and 20% is visible but partially see-through.

Practice Exercise 24 - Magic Eraser

File Menu→Open→C:\Data\PhotoshopCC-2\Balloons.jpg→ Open .
Select the Magic Eraser Tool→Erase the balloons.

2.23 Slice Tool

This allows you to split or divide an image into rectangular areas or **Slices**. Each of these areas, or **Slices**, can then be used to create links, rollovers, or animation in a web page containing an image.

2.23-1 Slice Tool Options

The following are the **Slice Tool** options located just under **Menus** on top of the interface:

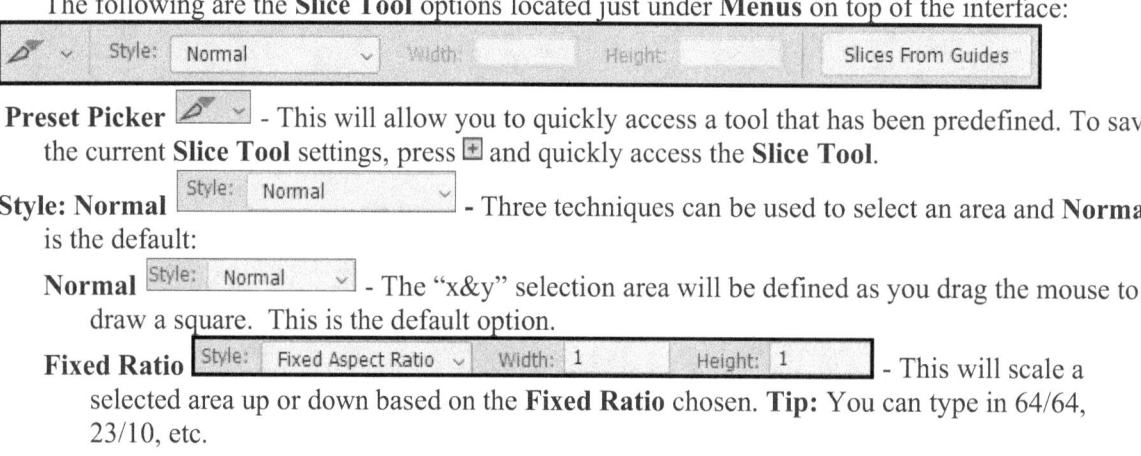

Preset Picker - This will allow you to quickly access a tool that has been predefined. To save the current **Slice Tool** settings, press ⊞ and quickly access the **Slice Tool**.

Style: Normal - Three techniques can be used to select an area and **Normal** is the default:

Normal - The "x&y" selection area will be defined as you drag the mouse to draw a square. This is the default option.

Fixed Ratio - This will scale a selected area up or down based on the **Fixed Ratio** chosen. **Tip:** You can type in 64/64, 23/10, etc.

Fixed Size - This will define a selection area to be the exact **Size** of the measurement used. The **Width** and **Height** option will enter the exact **Width/Height. Tip:** You can type in 23 Pixels, 2 inches.

Slices From Guides - This will create **Slices** based on defined **Guides**. **To add a guide go to:** *View Menu→ Rulers →Drag the Guide from the Ruler.* **To turn on the Guides:** *View Menu→Show→Guides.*

2.24 Slice Select Tool

This is used to select individual **Slices** or parts of an image that have been divided using the **Slice Tool**. When elements of an image overlap, it is easier to select a particular element using the **Slicer Select Tool**. Hold the **Ctrl** key down and select a portion of the image.

2.24-1 Slice Select Tool Options

The following are the **Slice Select Tool** options located just under **Menus** on top of the interface:

Chapter 2 - In-Depth Drawing Tools

Preset Picker - This will allow you to quickly access a tool that has been predefined. To save the current **Slice Select Tool** settings, press ⊞ and quickly access the **Slice Select Tool**.

Bring To Front - If **Slices** overlap, a specific **Slice** will be brought to the front of all **Slices**.

Bring Forward - If **Slices** overlap, a specific **Slice Forward** will be brought to one level.

Send Backward - If **Slices** overlap, **Slice Backward** will push a specific **Slice Backward** one level.

Send To Back - If **Slices** overlap, a specific **Slice** will be pushed to the back of all **Slices**.

Promote - If a **Slice** label is grayed out, the **Promote** button will convert it to what is called a **User Slice.** This provides greater editing and adjustment capability.

Divide - Use this option if you want to create evenly spaced and aligned **Slices**. You must choose **Promote** to convert to a **User Slice** in order to **Divide** it.

Align Options:

    Vertical Alignment - This will **Align** the selected objects placed in different layers **Vertically.**

    Horizontal Alignment - This will **Align** the selected objects placed in different layers **Horizontally.**

    Distribute - This will **Distribute** objects placed in different layers **Vertically** or **Horizontally**.

    Distribute Spacing - This will evenly space objects placed on different layers **Vertically** or **Horizontally**.

Show/Hide Auto Slices - This will **Hide** some markers associated with **Slices**.

Slice Options - This will allow you to define the **Name, URL, Target, Message Text, Alt Tag,** and **Dimensions** of a specific **Slice.**

Practice Exercise 25 - Slice

Use the **Slice Tool** to slice a rectangle around the brownies:

1. *File Menu →Open →C:\Data\PhotoshopCC-2\Browines.png →* Open .
2. *Slice Tool →Draw a rectangle around the brownies.*
3. *Slice Select Tool →Double click on the brownies →* OK
4. *File Menu →Save for the web →Save button (on the lower right corner) →Format: Images Only →Save →Save it in the PhotoshopCC-2 folder.*

Tip: The images will be sliced up and stored in the Images folder.

2.25 Brush Defaults

This will allow you to change the order of the **Brushes** that appear in the **Brush** dropdown. Go to: *Brush Tool → Window Menu → Brush Presets → Open Preset Manager Icon on the bottom of the Panel → Move brushes to reorder → Done.*

To view the results: *Brush Tool options → Press the down arrow.*

2.26 Add New Brushes

This will allow you to add **Brush Patterns** to the library.

To add more brushes: *Brush Tool → Brush Presets Panel → Brush Presets Panel Menu (upper right corner) → Choose a new preset → Append.*

2.27 Create New Brushes

These are new **Brush Styles** that can be created in the **Brush Settings Panel**.

To add new Brush Styles: Go to *Brush Tool → Window Menu → Brush → Modify the settings:*

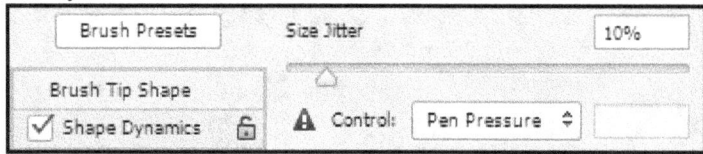

→Create Brush Icon → Enter new name: My Brush → OK .

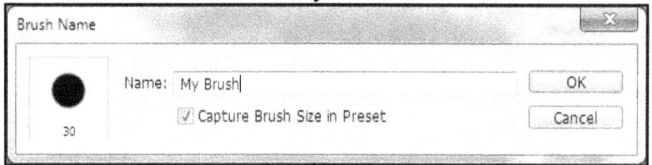

"My Brush" is located in the Brush options dropdown list (**Brush Presets**).

Chapter 3 - Touch-Up Images

This important aspect of **Photoshop** allows for the repairing of flaws, glitches, and damaged photos. The included tools are called "**Healing Tools**" because pixels are mixed with other surrounding pixels to provide a smoothing and blending effect.

Chapter Table Of Contents

3.1 Crop Tool
3.2 Spot Healing Brush Tool
3.3 Healing Brush Tool
3.4 Patch Tool
3.5 Redeye Tool
3.6 Clone Stamp Tool
3.7 Blur Tool
3.8 Sharpen Tool
3.9 Smudge Tool
3.10 Dodge Tool
3.11 Burn Tool
3.12 Sponge Tool

3.1 Crop Tool

This tool will reduce or expand the outer pixels around an image. It can be used to identify a specific object in an image and also to straighten angled pictures. Furthermore, it can be used to eliminate white borders from scanned images. *Crop Tool →Select area to be cropped→ Adjust crop area and angle →Press the Commit button or press the* Enter *key.*

3.1-1 Crop Tool Options

The following are the **Crop Tool** options located just under **Menus** on top of the interface:

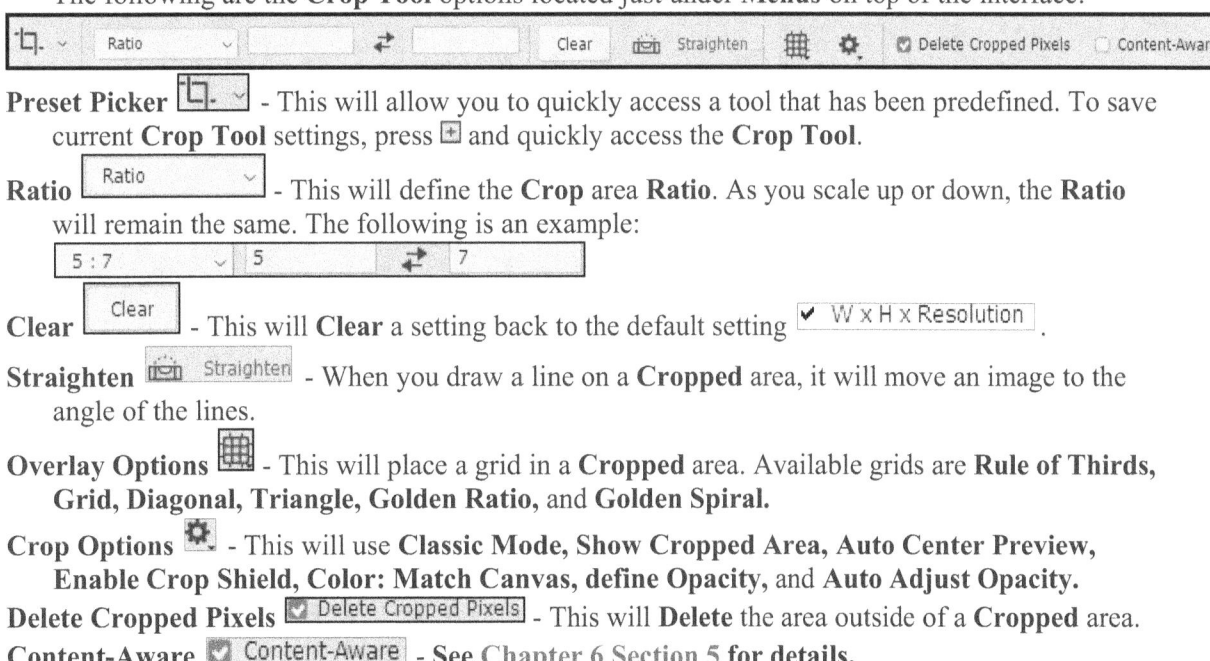

Preset Picker - This will allow you to quickly access a tool that has been predefined. To save current **Crop Tool** settings, press and quickly access the **Crop Tool**.

Ratio - This will define the **Crop** area **Ratio**. As you scale up or down, the **Ratio** will remain the same. The following is an example:

Clear - This will **Clear** a setting back to the default setting W x H x Resolution.

Straighten - When you draw a line on a **Cropped** area, it will move an image to the angle of the lines.

Overlay Options - This will place a grid in a **Cropped** area. Available grids are **Rule of Thirds, Grid, Diagonal, Triangle, Golden Ratio,** and **Golden Spiral.**

Crop Options - This will use **Classic Mode, Show Cropped Area, Auto Center Preview, Enable Crop Shield, Color: Match Canvas, define Opacity,** and **Auto Adjust Opacity.**

Delete Cropped Pixels - This will **Delete** the area outside of a **Cropped** area.

Content-Aware - See Chapter 6 Section 5 for details.

Practice Exercise 26 - Move to file

File Menu→Open→ C:\Data\PhotoshopCC-2\Cups And Mugs Flyer.jpg→ Open *.*

Crop Tool →Draw a box around a Mug → Press the check in the Crop options on the top of the screen.

Chapter 3 - Touch-Up Images

3.2 Spot Healing Brush Tool

This will fix a blemished area by pulling an unblemished area outside of an affected portion.
Spot Healing Brush Tool→Click the affected area.

3.1-1 Spot Healing Brush Tool Options

The following are the **Spot Healing Brush Tool** options located just under **Menus** on top of the interface:

Preset Picker - This will allow you to quickly access a tool that has been predefined. To save the current **Crop Tool** settings, press ⊞ and quickly access the **Crop Tool**.

Brush Characteristics:

Brush Size: →*Brush Preset Picker dropdown* →.

Brush Hardness: →*Brush Preset Picker dropdown* →.

Brushes: →*Brush Preset Picker dropdown* →.

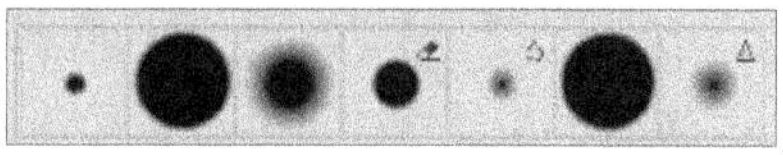

Painting Mode - Oftentimes, a **Mode** will blend with colors behind a blemished area. The most commonly used **Modes** include **Color Burn, Linear Dodge, Vivid Light, Linear Light, Hard Mix,** and **Difference**.

Content-Aware - See Chapter 6 Section 5 for details.

Create Texture - When you take a sample, this will generate a **Texture** pattern. Then, it uses this pattern to blend in with the area being modified. This is the default setting.

Proximity Match - This mode repairs and blends using actual pixels rather than blending using the **Texture** pattern.

Sample All Layers - This will identify applied web paint from **All Layers**.

Pencil Angle - This will set an **Angle** as you begin to draw. However, this is not noticeable in normal situations.

Pressure For Size - Always use **Pressure For Size**. When turned off, **Brush Preset** controls **Pressure** and works best with a tablet pen rather than a mouse.

Practice Exercise 27 - Spot Healing Brush

1. ***File Menu→Open→Filename: C:\Data\Photoshopcc-2\Thomas Jefferson Memorial.jpg→*** Open.
2. ***Create a new layer: Click the*** ⊞ ***Create A New Layer located at the bottom of the Layers Panel.***
3. ***Select a new layer→Spot Healing Brush Tool→Start drawing over the Airplane.***

Chapter 3 - Touch-Up Images

4. *Spot Healing changes are now on the new layer.*
5. *Turn off the ◉ Eye icon in front of a New layer to see the original image.*

3.3 Healing Brush Tool

This provides natural-looking touch-ups that are not uniform in color or texture. It also corrects or repairs imperfections by sampling an image or pattern. *Healing Brush Tool → Hold the* Alt *key and sample just above the imperfection → Click the blemished area several times or drag and draw.*
Mac CS6: *Use the* option *key*.

3.3-1 Healing Brush Tool Options

The following are the **Healing Brush Tool** options located just under **Menus** on top of the interface:

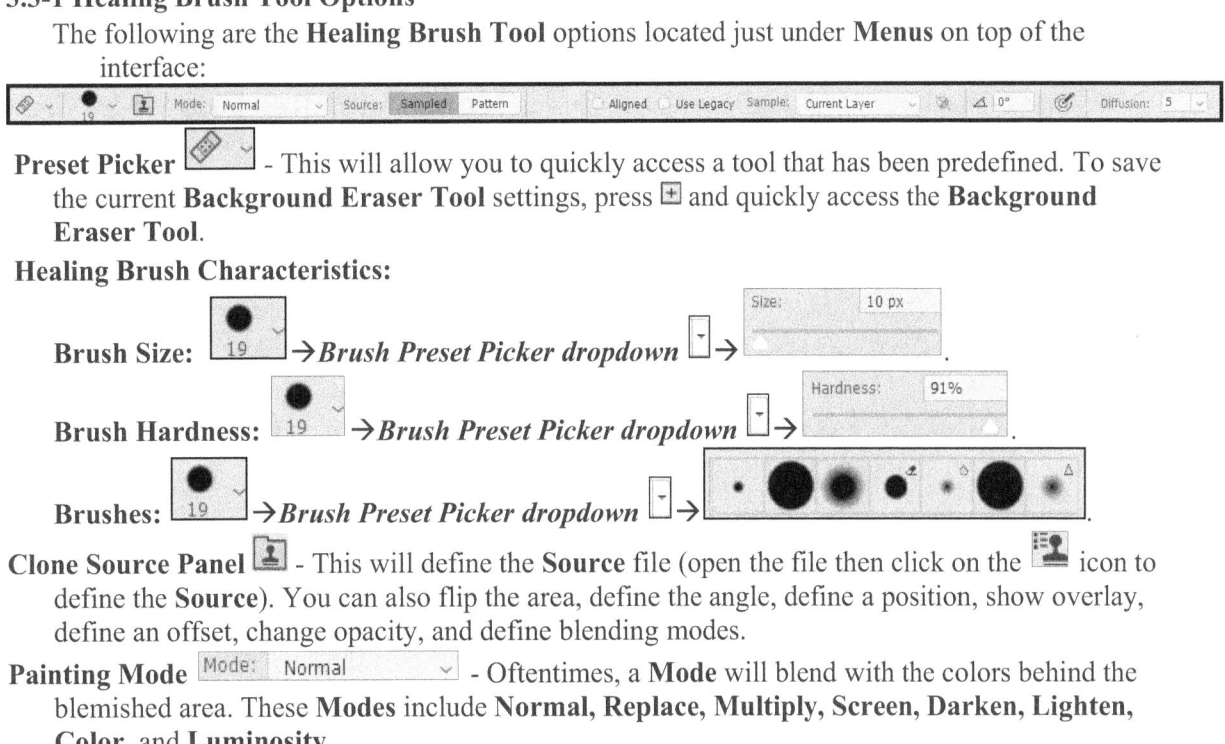

Preset Picker - This will allow you to quickly access a tool that has been predefined. To save the current **Background Eraser Tool** settings, press ⊞ and quickly access the **Background Eraser Tool**.

Healing Brush Characteristics:

Brush Size: → *Brush Preset Picker dropdown* →.

Brush Hardness: → *Brush Preset Picker dropdown* →.

Brushes: → *Brush Preset Picker dropdown* →.

Clone Source Panel - This will define the **Source** file (open the file then click on the icon to define the **Source**). You can also flip the area, define the angle, define a position, show overlay, define an offset, change opacity, and define blending modes.

Painting Mode - Oftentimes, a **Mode** will blend with the colors behind the blemished area. These **Modes** include **Normal, Replace, Multiply, Screen, Darken, Lighten, Color,** and **Luminosity.**

Source Sampled - This sets a **Source** by **Sampling** a location on the canvas in order to repair a damaged area.

Source Pattern - This sets a **Pattern** as the **Source** in order to repair a damaged area.

Aligned - This will **Align** each stroke side by side even if you begin the second stroke in a different position. If it is unchecked, random strokes will be the result.

Use Legacy - This will turn on the **Legacy** algorithm defined in **Photoshop CC (2014)**.

Sample - **Options** available include **Current Layer, Current & Below,** and **All Layers.**

Ignore Adjustment Layers - By default, this is turned on and will **Ignore Adjustments** applied to **Layers**.

Pencil Angle - This will set an **Angle** as you begin to draw. However, this is not noticeable in normal situations.

Pressure For Size - Always use **Pressure For Size**. When turned off, **Brush Preset** controls **Pressure**. This works best with a tablet pen rather than a mouse.

Diffusion [Diffusion: 5] - This will control how quickly a pasted region adapts to an image area. A low slider value is better for most images with detail, but high values will work best with smoother images containing less detail.

Practice Exercise 28 - Healing Brush Tool

Test out the above tools by applying the **Red Eye Tool** to the eyes.
1. *File Menu→Open→C:\Data\PhotoshopCC-2\Tony's First Communion.jpg→* [Open].
2. *Healing Brush Tool→ Hold the* [Alt] *key and sample just above the imperfection→Click the blemished area several times or drag and draw.*

3.4 Patch Tool

Here, a bad area interacts with a "good" area and eventually blends the imperfections. This tool helps to match texture, lighting, and shading around edges to repair a selected area.

3.4-1 Patch Tool Options - When you select the **Patch Tool** options, the options will appear just under the **Menus** on the top of the interface:

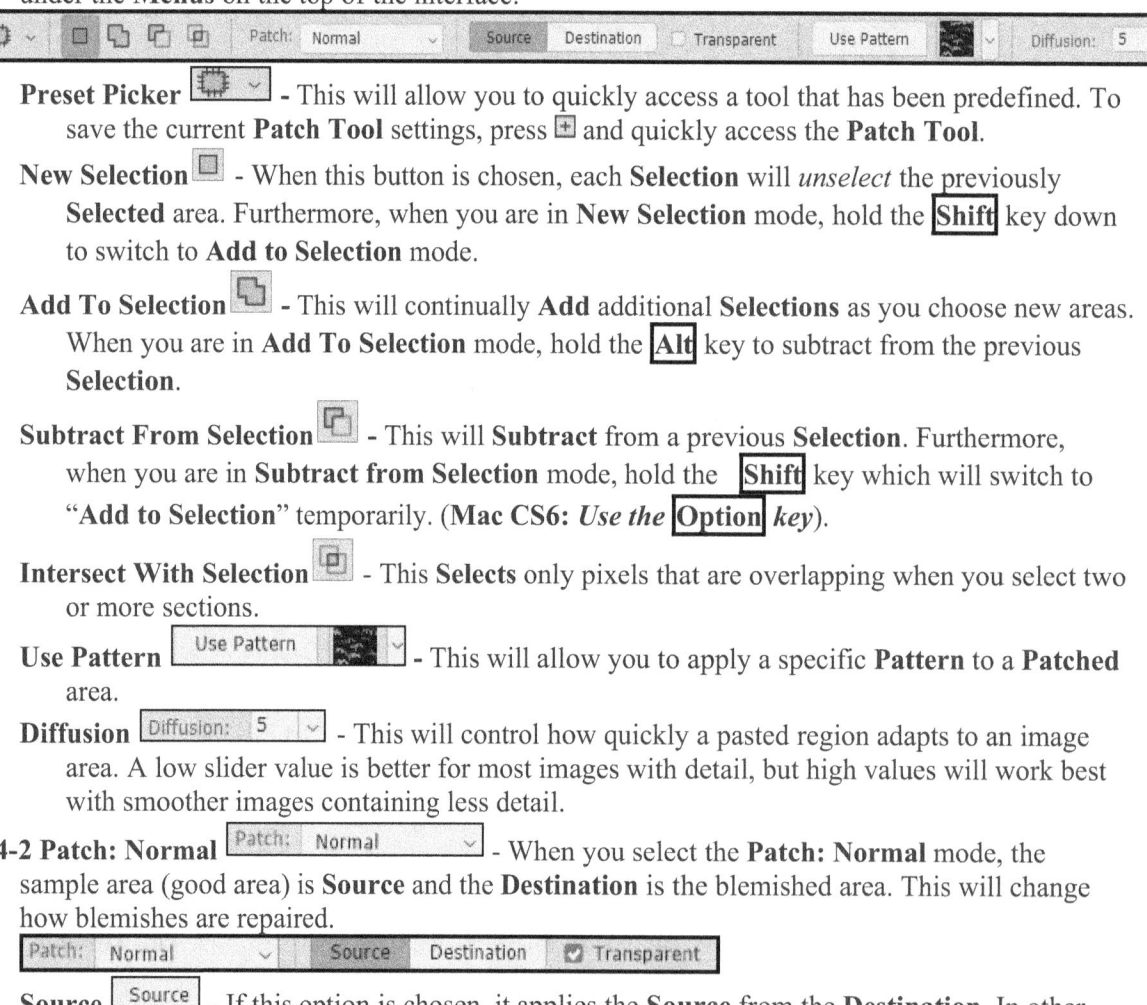

Preset Picker - This will allow you to quickly access a tool that has been predefined. To save the current **Patch Tool** settings, press [+] and quickly access the **Patch Tool**.

New Selection - When this button is chosen, each **Selection** will *unselect* the previously **Selected** area. Furthermore, when you are in **New Selection** mode, hold the [Shift] key down to switch to **Add to Selection** mode.

Add To Selection - This will continually **Add** additional **Selections** as you choose new areas. When you are in **Add To Selection** mode, hold the [Alt] key to subtract from the previous **Selection**.

Subtract From Selection - This will **Subtract** from a previous **Selection**. Furthermore, when you are in **Subtract from Selection** mode, hold the [Shift] key which will switch to "**Add to Selection**" temporarily. (**Mac CS6:** *Use the* [Option] *key*).

Intersect With Selection - This **Selects** only pixels that are overlapping when you select two or more sections.

Use Pattern - This will allow you to apply a specific **Pattern** to a **Patched** area.

Diffusion [Diffusion: 5] - This will control how quickly a pasted region adapts to an image area. A low slider value is better for most images with detail, but high values will work best with smoother images containing less detail.

3.4-2 Patch: Normal - When you select the **Patch: Normal** mode, the sample area (good area) is **Source** and the **Destination** is the blemished area. This will change how blemishes are repaired.

Source - If this option is chosen, it applies the **Source** from the **Destination**. In other words, when you select a blemished area (**Destination**) and move it to the sample area (**Source**), the blemish area (**Destination**) will be fixed.

Chapter 3 - Touch-Up Images

Destination [Destination] - If this option is chosen, it applies the **Destination** from the **Source**. In other words, when you select the good area (**Source**) and move it to the blemished area (**Destination**), the blemish area (**Destination**) will be repaired.

Transparent [☑ Transparent] - This option will allow a **Patched** area to apply fewer pixels to repair a blemished area.

3.4-3 Patch: Content-Aware [Patch: Content-Aware ˅] - When you select the "**Patch: Content-Aware**" mode, structure and **Color** options are available.

[Patch: Content-Aware Structure: 4 ˅ Color: 0 ˅]

Structure: 4 [Structure: 4 ˅] - The higher the number, the more **Source Structure** is preserved, or more of a sample area is applied. However, the lower the number, the less **Source Structure** is preserved and becomes more mixed or blurry.

Color: 0 [Color: 0 ˅] - The higher the number, the more of the **Source Color** or sample area **Source Color** is applied. The lower the number, the less **Source Color** is applied.

Practice Exercise 29 - Patch Tool

Patch Tool →X Source →O Transparent →Draw a circle around the Imperfection →Drag the selected area into an unblemished area.

3.5 Redeye Tool

[icon] This tool removes **Red** from an **Eye** within an image. However, the **Redeye Tool** is no longer necessary because this problem is not created by newer cameras today.

3.5-1 Redeye Tool Options - When you select the **Redeye Tool**, options will appear under **Menus** on the top of the interface:

[+⊙ ˅   Pupil Size: 50% ˅   Darken Amount: 50% ˅]

Preset Picker [+⊙ ˅] - This will allow you to quickly access a tool that has been predefined. To save the current **Redeye Tool** settings, press ⊞ and quickly access the **Redeye Tool**.

Pupil Size [Pupil Size: 50% ˅] - This will change how much of an area will be darkened using pixels in the center of the **Eye**.

Darken Amount [Darken Amount: 50% ˅] - This will increase or decrease **Darkening** colors.

Practice Exercise 30 - Redeye

File Menu →Open →C:\Data\PhotoshopCC-2\Red-eye.jpg → [Open].
Red Eye Tool →Click in the red area. Available in CS2.

3.6 Clone Stamp Tool

[icon] This samples parts of an image by pressing the [Alt] key. It paints a sample over imperfections. (**Mac:** *Use the* [Option] *key*). [Alt] *key →Select area outside the imperfection →Paint over imperfection.* **Mac CS6:** *Use the* [option] *key.*

3.6-1 Clone Stamp Tool Features:

1. **Add additional Brushes:** *Brush options* [50] *→Brush Preset Picker dropdown* [˅] *→ Brush Preset Picker Menu* ⚙ *(top Right side) to choose additional brush Styles such as Append Default Brushes or Legacy Brushes.*

2. **Cursor Style** - Press the **Caps Lock** key to change the **Cursor** to a more precise drawing layout. **Caps Lock/off** is a circle and **Caps Lock/on** is a cross with a dot.

3.6-2 Clone Stamp Tool Options

The following are the **Clone Stamp Tool** options located just under **Menus** on top of the interface:

Preset Picker - This will allow you to quickly access a tool that has been predefined. To save the current **Clone Stamp Tool** settings, press and quickly access the **Clone Stamp Tool**.

Clone Stamp Brush Characteristics:

Brush Size: → *Brush Preset Picker dropdown* →

Brush Hardness: → *Brush Preset Picker dropdown* →

Brushes: → *Brush Preset Picker dropdown* →

Brush Settings Panel - This will toggle the **Brush Settings Panel**.

Clone Source Panel - This will define the **Source** file (open the file then click on the icon to define the **Source**). You can also flip the area, define the angle, define a position, show overlay, define an offset, change opacity, and define blending modes.

Painting Mode - Oftentimes, a **Mode** will blend with colors behind a stroke. The most commonly used **Modes** include **Color Burn, Linear Dodge, Vivid Light, Linear Light, Hard Mix,** and **Difference**.

Opacity 100% - The **Brush Stroke** is more see-through or transparent. Solid is 100%, 0% is see-through, and 20% is visible but partially see-through.

Pressure for Opacity - The **Opacity** will change depending on the amount of **Pressure** applied using a tablet pen (not a mouse). When turned off, **Brush Preset** controls **Pressure**.

Flow - This is a percentage that sets the rate of color applied or the amount of ink that is applied to the tool.

Airbrush - This simulates painting with an **Airbrush**.

Clone Angle - This will set an **Angle** as you begin to draw. It is not noticeable in normal situations.

Aligned - This will **Align** each stroke side by side even if you begin the second stroke in a different position. If it is unchecked, will contain random strokes.

Clone Sample Mode - **Options** available include **Current Layer, Current & Below,** and **All Layers.**

Adjustment Layers - **Adjustment Layers** will be ignored when being cloned

Pressure For Size - Always use **Pressure For Size**. When turned off, **Brush Preset** controls **Pressure** and this works best with a tablet pen rather than a mouse.

Tip: If you create a new layer after sampling an area, it will paint the imperfection on the new blank layer.

Chapter 3 - Touch-Up Images

Practice Exercise 31 - Clone Stamp Blank Layer

1. *Use the opened file "Thomas Jefferson Memorial.jpg."*
2. *Clone the Monument next to the existing monument.*
3. *Hold the Alt key and click the corner of the roof.*
4. *Let go of the Alt key.*
5. *Create a new layer: Click the ☐ Create A New Layer located at the bottom of the Layers Panel.*
6. *Begin drawing to the right side of the Monument to create another image.*

Practice Exercise 32 - Clone Stamp Same Layer

1. *Use the opened file "Thomas Jefferson Memorial.jpg."*
2. *Clone the Monument next to the existing monument.*
3. *Hold the Alt key and click the corner of the roof.*
4. *Let go of the Alt key and begin drawing to the right side of the Monument to create another image.*

3.7 Blur Tool

This smooths wrinkles of a face or **Blurs** edges. It does not mix pixel colors.
Select area→Blur Tool→Paint over the area.

3.7-1 Blur Tool Options

The following are the **Blur Tool** options located under **Menus** on top of the interface:

Preset Picker - This will allow you to quickly access a tool that has been predefined. To save the current **Blur Tool** settings, press ☐ and quickly access the **Blur Tool**.

Blur Tool Brush Characteristics:

Brush Size: →*Brush Preset Picker dropdown*.

Brush Hardness: →*Brush Preset Picker dropdown*.

Brushes: →*Brush Preset Picker dropdown*.

Brush Settings Panel - This toggles or opens the **Brush Settings Panel** or press: *Window Menu→Brush*.

Mode Normal - Oftentimes, a **Mode** will blend the colors behind a brush stroke. **Tip:** Draw using **Hard light** vs. **Vivid Light** to see differences.

Strength - The higher the **Strength** the tool will become more **Blurry**.

Blur Angle - This will set an **Angle** as you start to draw. It is not noticeable in normal situations.

Sample All Layers - This will identify the applied web paint for **All Layers**.

Pressure For Size - Always use **Pressure For Size**. When turned off, **Brush Preset** controls **Pressure** and works best with a tablet pen rather than a mouse.

Chapter 3 - Touch-Up Images

3.8 Sharpen Tool

This makes an image clearer and **Sharpens** edges. *Select area →Sharpen Tool →Paint area slowly.*

3.8-1 Sharpen Tool Options

The following are the **Sharpen Tool** options located under **Menus** on top of the interface:

Preset Picker - This will allow you to quickly access a tool that has been predefined. To save the current **Sharpen Tool** settings, press and quickly access **Sharpen Tool**.

Blur Tool Brush Characteristics:

Brush Size: →*Brush Preset Picker dropdown* →

Brush Hardness: →*Brush Preset Picker dropdown* →

Brushes: →*Brush Preset Picker dropdown* →

Brush Settings Panel - This will toggle the **Brush Settings Panel**.

Mode Normal - Oftentimes, a mode will blend with the colors behind a brush stroke. **Tip:** Draw using **Hard light** vs. **Vivid Light** to see differences.

Strength - The higher the **Strength,** the tool will become more **Sharpened**.

Blur Angle - This will set an **Angle** when you begin to draw. It is not noticeable in normal situations.

Sample All Layers - This will identify applied web paint for **All Layers**.

Protect Details - This should be checked because it **Protects** an image from producing lower quality after **Sharpening** has been applied.

Pressure For Size - Always use **Pressure For Size**. When turned off, **Brush Preset** controls **Pressure** and works best with a tablet pen rather than a mouse.

Practice Exercise 33 - Open Flowering Branch

File Menu →Open →C:\Data\PhotoshopCC-2\Flowering Branch.jpg → 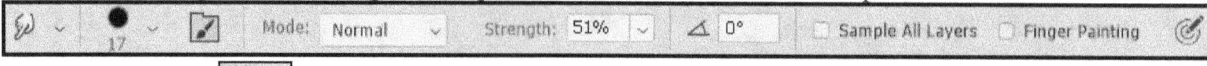.

3.9 Smudge Tool

This distorts a selected area. Sometimes, the result is as if someone has drug their finger across wet paint. *Select area →Smudge Tool →Draw area.*

3.9-1 Smudge Tool Options

The following are the **Smudge Tool** options located under **Menus** on top of the interface:

Preset Picker - This will allow you to quickly access a tool that has been predefined. To save the current **Smudge Tool** settings, press and quickly access the **Smudge Tool**.

Smudge Brush Characteristics:

Chapter 3 - Touch-Up Images

Brush Size: →*Brush Preset Picker dropdown* →.

Brush Hardness: →*Brush Preset Picker dropdown* →.

Brushes: →*Brush Preset Picker dropdown* →.

Brush Settings Panel - This will toggle the **Brush Settings Panel**.

Mode Normal - Oftentimes, a **Mode** will blend with colors behind a brush stroke. **Tip:** Draw using **Hard light** vs. **Vivid Light** to see differences.

Strength - The higher the **Strength** of the tool, the more **Smudge** will occur.

Blur Angle - This will set an **Angle** as you begin to draw. It is not noticeable in normal situations.

Sample All Layers - This will identify applied web paint from **All Layers**.

Finger Painting - This will allow you to use your **Finger** on a touch-screen to **Paint** a foreground color.

Pressure For Size - Always use **Pressure For Size**. When turned off, **Brush Preset** controls **Pressure** and works best with a tablet pen rather than a mouse.

3.10 Dodge Tool

This brightens up an image. *Select area → Dodge Tool → Paint area.*

3.10-1 Dodge Tool Options

The following are the **Dodge Tool** options located under **Menus** on top of the interface:

Preset Picker - This will allow you to quickly access a tool that has been predefined. To save the current **Smudge Tool** settings, press and quickly access the **Smudge Tool**.

Dodge Brush Characteristics:

Brush Size: →*Brush Preset Picker dropdown* →.

Brush Hardness: →*Brush Preset Picker dropdown* →.

Brushes: →*Brush Preset Picker dropdown* →.

Brush Settings Panel - This will toggle the **Brush Settings Panel**.

Range: Midtones - This will allow you to apply **Highlights**, **Midtones,** or **Shadows** to an area being painted with the **Dodge Tool.**

Exposure - The higher the percentage, an indicated area will provide greater **Exposure**. The lower the percentage, the less **Exposure** will be applied.

Airbrush - This simulates painting with an **Airbrush**.

Dodge Angle - This will set an **Angle** as you begin to draw. It is not noticeable in normal situations.

Chapter 3 - Touch-Up Images

Protect Tones ☑ Protect Tones - This minimizes clipping in shadows and highlights.

Pressure For Size - Always use **Pressure For Size**. When turned off, **Brush Preset** controls **Pressure** and works best with a tablet pen rather than a mouse.

3.11 Burn Tool

This darkens the highlights. *Select area→Burn Tool→Paint area.*

3.11-1 Burn Tool Options

The following are the **Burn Tool** options located under **Menus** on top of the interface:

Preset Picker - This will allow you to quickly access a tool that has been predefined. To save the current **Burn Tool** settings, press ⊞ and quickly access the **Burn Tool**.

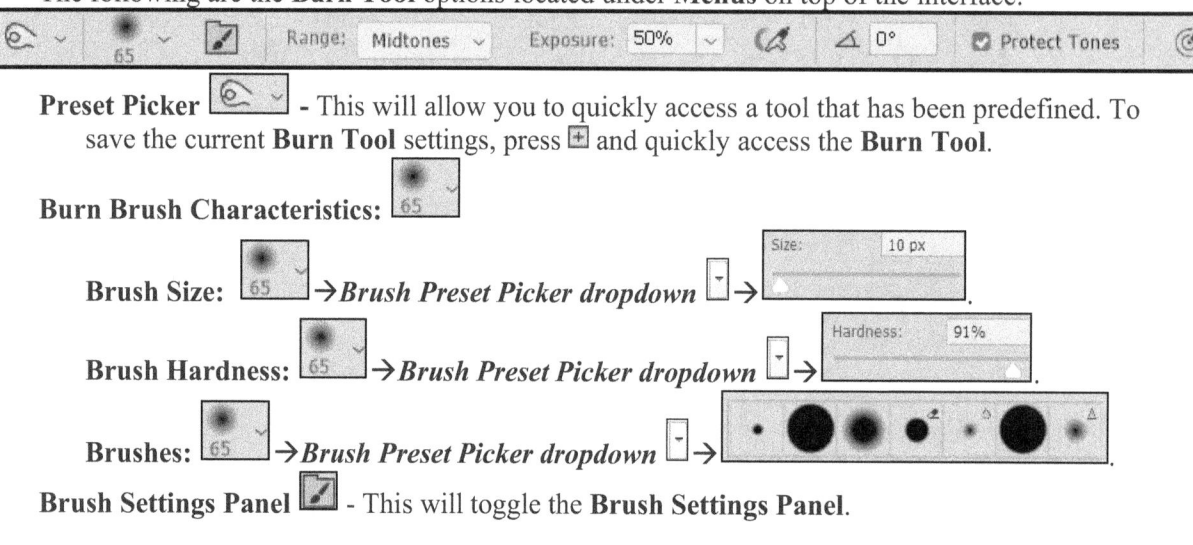

Burn Brush Characteristics:

Brush Size: →*Brush Preset Picker dropdown* →

Brush Hardness: →*Brush Preset Picker dropdown* →

Brushes: →*Brush Preset Picker dropdown* →

Brush Settings Panel - This will toggle the **Brush Settings Panel**.

Range: Midtones - This will allow you to apply **Highlights**, **Midtones**, or **Shadows** to an area you are painting with the **Burn Tool.**

Exposure - The higher the percentage, the indicated area will provide greater **Exposure.** The lower the percentage, the less **Exposure** will be applied.

Airbrush - This simulates painting with an **Airbrush.**

Dodge Angle - This will set an **Angle** as you begin to draw. It is not noticeable in normal situations.

Protect Tones ☑ Protect Tones - This will protect your shadows and highlights from shifting to a closer hue color.

Pressure For Size - Always use **Pressure For Size**. When turned off, **Brush Preset** controls **Pressure** and works best with a tablet pen rather than a mouse.

3.12 Sponge Tool

This puts a film on an area, adds color, or can also be used to saturate. It also brightens and enhances the color. *Select area→Sponge Tool→Paint area.*

3.12-1 Sponge Tool Options

The following are the **Sponge Tool** options located under **Menus** on top of the interface:

Preset Picker - This will allow you to quickly access a tool that has been predefined. To save the current **Sponge Tool** settings, press ⊞ and quickly access the **Sponge Tool**.

Chapter 3 - Touch-Up Images

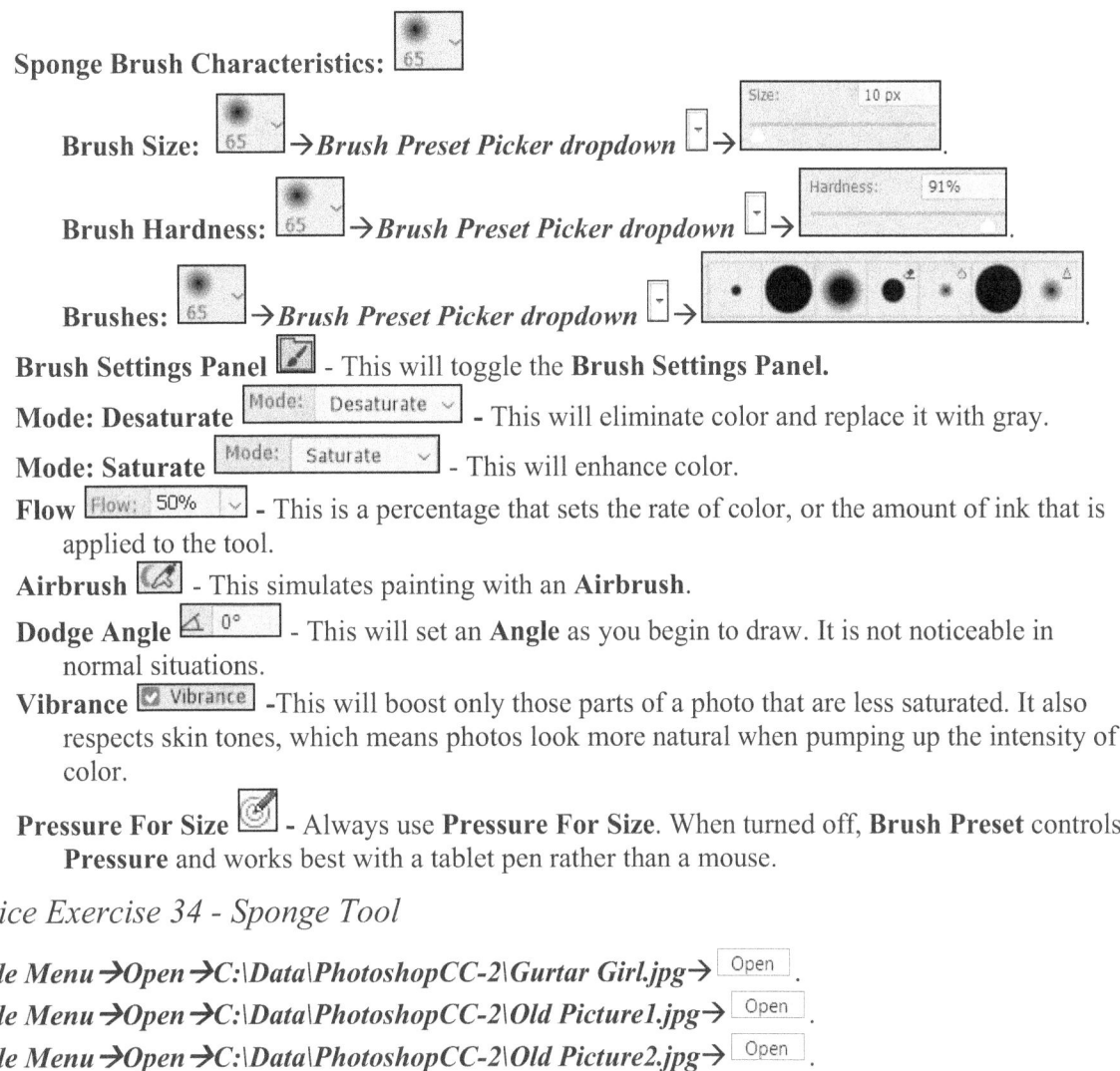

Sponge Brush Characteristics:

Brush Size: → *Brush Preset Picker dropdown* →.

Brush Hardness: → *Brush Preset Picker dropdown* →.

Brushes: → *Brush Preset Picker dropdown* →.

Brush Settings Panel - This will toggle the **Brush Settings Panel.**

Mode: Desaturate - This will eliminate color and replace it with gray.

Mode: Saturate - This will enhance color.

Flow - This is a percentage that sets the rate of color, or the amount of ink that is applied to the tool.

Airbrush - This simulates painting with an **Airbrush**.

Dodge Angle - This will set an **Angle** as you begin to draw. It is not noticeable in normal situations.

Vibrance -This will boost only those parts of a photo that are less saturated. It also respects skin tones, which means photos look more natural when pumping up the intensity of color.

Pressure For Size - Always use **Pressure For Size**. When turned off, **Brush Preset** controls **Pressure** and works best with a tablet pen rather than a mouse.

Practice Exercise 34 - Sponge Tool

File Menu →Open →C:\Data\PhotoshopCC-2\Gurtar Girl.jpg→ Open .

File Menu →Open →C:\Data\PhotoshopCC-2\Old Picture1.jpg→ Open .

File Menu →Open →C:\Data\PhotoshopCC-2\Old Picture2.jpg→ Open .

Chapter 3 - Touch-Up Images

Student Project B - Touch-Up Images

Step 1: Open the file indicated below (located in the *C:\Data\PhotoshopCC-2* **folder**).
Step 2: Make multiple-layer copies of the active layer *Select Layer →Layer Menu →Layer via Copy*.
Step 3: Use the suggested tools on each layer (suggestions 1, 2, 3, 4, etc).
Step 4: Compare differences by turning off the layers.

Problem With Image	Example Files	Crop	Spot Healing Brush	Healing Brush	Patch	Red-Eye	Clone Stamp	Blur	Sharpen	Smudge	Dodge	Burn	Sponge	Clone Stamp
Correct angled pictures.	Gondola.jpg	1							2					
Correct angled pictures.	Leaning House.jpg	1								3				2
Imperfections	Ancestors.jpg		3	2	1		4							
Remove a text stamp on a picture.	Tara Nate.jpg		4	2	1		3							
Fix photodamage.	Old Image.png		1	2			3							
Improve Pictures	Rock Climb.jpg		1	2	4		3							
Torn Pictures	Canoe Race.jpg			3	4		2							
Redeye - Removes red	Red-eye Girl.jpg Red-eye Boy.png					1								
Brightens up a specified color.	Canoe Boy.jpg												1	
Smooths the wrinkles of a face.	Face Wrinkles.jpg							1		2				
Sharpen picture details.	Spice Display.jpg							1	2		1	3	4	

Page 46

Chapter 4 - Advanced Layers

We will begin by discussing a few of the special **Layer** features and adjusting **Layers**.

Chapter Contents:
    Section 1: Layer Panel Options
    Section 2: Visible Layers
    Section 3: Layer Menu
    Section 4: Layer Manipulation

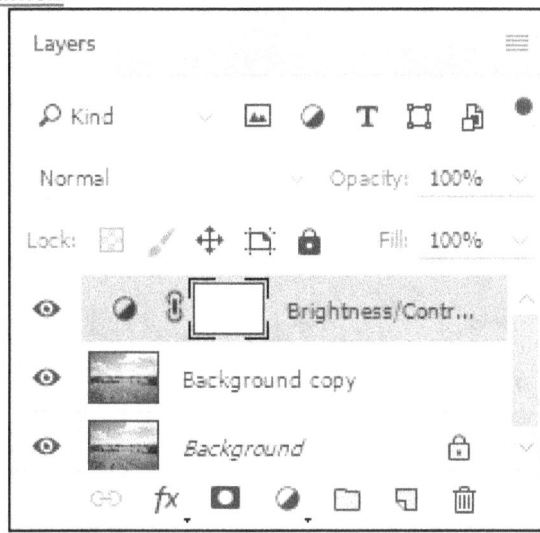

Section 1: Layer Panel Options

These options are located on the top three rows of the **Layers Panel** which can be opened by: *Window→Layers.*

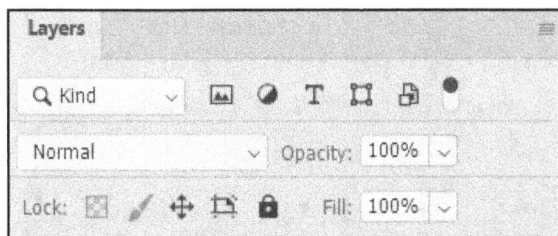

Also, some icons are located at the bottom of the **Layers Panel**:

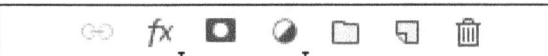

Practice Exercise 35 - Open Mountain trail.jpg
    Use the following file to test features in this section.
    File Menu→Open→C:\Data\PhotoshopCC-2\Mountain Trail.jpg→ Open .
Tip: Alternate files to open: **sea cliff.jpg** or **harbor.jpg** or **Sunlight Detergent.psd.**

4.1 Layer Filter

Layer display options are located on the top row of the **Layers Panel** and icons are discussed from left to right. Press the dropdown arrow next to the word "**Kind**".

Page 47

Chapter 4 - Advanced Layers

4.1-1 Kind [Q Kind] [□ ● T ☐ ⊞] - This is the default option and will display any **Layer** that contains the following attributes:

Image ▦ - This will display normal raster **Photoshop Layers** within the **Layers Panel**.

Adjustment ● - This will display **Layers** that have been **Adjusted** using the ● **Adjustment** icon located on the bottom of the **Layers Panel**.

Text T - This will display **Text Layers** created using the **T Type Tool.**

Shape ☐ -This will display **Layers** that have been created using the **Shapes Tool**.

Tip: The following **Shapes** are supported: **Rectangles** ▢, **Rounded Rectangles** ▢, **Ellipses** ◯, **Polygons** ⬡, **Lines** ╱, and **Custom Shapes** ✦.

Smart Object ⊞ - This will display **Layers** that have been placed using embedded objects. *File Menu→Place Embedded*.

4.1-2 Name [Q Name] [Layer1] - This will display by **Layer Name**.

4.1-3 Effect [Q Effect] [Bevel & Emboss] - This will display **Layers** that contain **Bevel & Emboss, Stroke, Inner Shadow, Inner Glow, Satin, Overlay, Outer Glow,** and **Drop Shadow**.

4.1-4 Mode [Q Mode] [Normal] - This will display any **Layer** that has a **Mode** applied to it.

4.1-5 Attribute [Q Attribute] [Visible] - This will display any **Layer** that has the following **Attributes** applied: **Visible, Locked, Empty, Linked, Clipped, Layer Mask, Vector Layer, Layer Effects, Advanced Blending, Not Visible, Not Locked, Not Empty, Not Linked, Not Clipped, No Layer Mask, No Vector Mask, No Layer Effects,** and **No Advanced Blending**.

4.1-6 Color [Q Color] [Red] - This will display any **Layer** that has a specific **Color** applied such as **Red, Orange, Yellow, Green Blue, Violet, Gray,** etc.

4.1-7 Smart Object [Q Smart Ob...] [▦ ⊞ ⚠ ❓ ⊞] - This will display a **Layer** that has a **Smart Object** applied such as: **Library Linked, Local Linked, Out of Date Linked, Missing Linked,** and **Embedded**.

4.1-8 Selected [Q Selected] - This will display any currently **Selected Layer**.

4.1-9 Artboard [Q Artboard] - This will display **Layers** applied to a specific **Artboard**.

4.2 Layer Blending Modes

This adjusts a selected **Layer** by adding a **non-destructive** film to brighten or darken a shadow over the **Layer**. These are non-destructive because you can delete **Blending Modes** by dragging them to the **Layer** 🗑 **Trash Bin**. One example of a darkening technique is "multiply" which provides shadows similar to a night effect. ***Press the dropdown arrow next to Normal*** [Normal]:

```
Normal
-------
Normal
Dissolve
-------
Darken
Multiply
Color Burn
Linear Burn
Darker Color
```

The most commonly used **Blending Modes** include:

Normal - This is the default with no blending.
Dissolve - This provides a speckled effect.
Darken - This will darken a **Layer**.

Page 48

Multiply - This darkens all colors so white will disappear.
Lighten - This displays the **Lightest** color of a selected **Layer**.
Screen - This brightens all colors and black disappears.
Overlay - This multiplies or increases a color shade depending on a base color. However, there is no effect on 50% gray.
Soft Light - This darkens or lightens color shades on a base color. However, there is no effect on 50% gray.
Color - This keeps the luminance of a base **Color** as well as the hue and saturation of the blend color.
Luminosity - This maintains the color of the base the same as well as the **Luminance** of the blend color.

4.3 Opacity

Opacity is used to make an image transparent. It can be applied over an entire layer, but some areas may need more to make an effect look more realistic. Effects that might need more **Opacity** include smoke, clouds, etc. It is common knowledge that 0% opacity is invisible, and 100% **Opacity** is full visibility. Therefore, **Transparency** is the opposite of **Opacity**. For example, 100% **Transparency** is invisible, and 0% **Transparency** is fully visible. **Opacity** will cast a shadow over an entire **Layer** by making it more clear. See **Fill** below to compare **Opacity** and **Fill** options.

4.4 Fill

The difference between **Opacity** and **Fill** on the **Layers Panel** is that **Opacity** will affect both objects and **Layer Styles**, but **Fill** only affects objects on a layer. In other words, if you apply a **Layer Style** (using the *fx* icon located on the bottom of the **Layers Panel**), the **Opacity** will apply more **Transparency** to the entire **Layer** including the **Layer Style**. However, the **Fill** will not affect elements that include **Layer Styles**.

4.5 Locked Layer

This **Locks** specific parts of a **Layer** from edits.
Locked Transparent Pixels - All **Transparent Pixels** will be **Locked**.
Lock Image Pixels - An original image is **Locked** to ensure it will not be damaged.
Lock Position - A **Locked Layer** cannot be moved.
Prevent Auto Nesting - This **Prevents Auto-nesting** into and out of **Artboards**.
Lock All - This **Locks** every aspect of a **Layer**.

4.6 Layer Style

The **Add A Layer Style** icon (located on the bottom of the **Layers Panel**) can affect a **Layer** in different ways. Results should be very subtle but should continue to enhance an image on the **Layer**. If it is grayed out, rename the **Background** Layer to **Layer 0**.

4.7 Layer Mask

This is similar to a face mask in that the white areas are visible, and the dark areas are hidden. In **Photoshop**, the selected area is visible and the area outside the selected area is invisible. This is located at the bottom of the **Layers Panel**.

4.8 Layer Adjustments

This will create a new **Adjustment Layer** on top of all layers (located on the bottom of the **Layers Panel**). The result will affect all **Layers** below the stack. Think of this as a special glass cover that you can see through or a filter that disguises the lower **Layers**. The film can be removed at a later time, if necessary, which makes it, then, a non-destructive **Layer** that will not affect main **Layers**.

4.9 New Layer

This creates a new blank **Layer** that can be used to create a new **Background Layer** (located at the bottom of the **Layers Panel**). Use the **Paint Bucket Tool** to color. Also, if you drag and drop a **Layer** to the ⊞ **New Layer** icon, it will create a duplicate.

Practice Exercise 36 - New Layer

1. *File Menu→Open→Sunlight Detergent.psd→* Open .
2. *Press the ⊞ New Layer icon (located in the lower-left corner of the Layers Panel).*
3. *Turn off the ⊙ Eye icon on all layers except the new layer.*
4. *Select the Paint Bucket Tool→Change the color to any desired color. Choose one of the following methods:*
   Swatches: *Window Menu→Swatches Panel.*
   Color: *Window Menu→Color.*
   Color Picker: *This is located at the bottom of the Tools (left side of the interface).*
5. *Using the left mouse button→Click in the middle of the New Layer located in the middle of the screen.*

4.10 Trash Can

This puts a **Layer** or mask in the **Trash Can** (located on the bottom of the **Layers Panel**).

Practice Exercise 37 - Trash Can

Continue from the previous practice exercise.

Drag several layers to the Trash Can (located in the lower right corner of the Layers Panel).

Section 2: Visible Layers

Practice Exercise 38 - New Layer

Open the following file to demonstrate these concepts.
1. *File Menu→Open→Allie Zack→* Open .

4.11 Layer Visibility

This will turn a **Layer** on or off and the image on the **Layer** will disappear. It can be used to identify an image on a **Layer** by turning the **Eye** on and off.

4.12 Background Layer

A **Background Layer** is special in that it will always remain at the bottom of a **Layer** stack. However, the **Background** must be renamed in order to manipulate it. **Double-click** on a **Background Layer** to rename it.

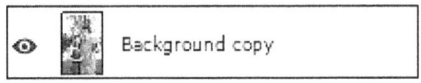

4.13 Raster Layers

Most photos are taken in a **Raster** format. As you adjust the resolution of a document, you will most likely lose pixels and/or lose resolution.

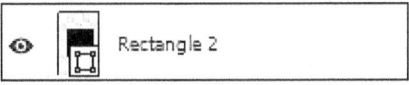

4.14 Shape Layers

This is a **Vector** layer created within **Photoshop** using a custom **Shape Tool**. As you scale up or down, you won't lose resolution because each object has a specific predefined size. Also, the lines and arcs in a **Vector Layer** can be modified.

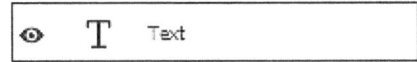

Practice Exercise 39 - Shape Layer

1. *File Menu →New → Print Presets →Letter (8.5 x 11 in @ 300 ppi →* Create.
2. *Select the Rectangle Shape Tool →Draw a Rectangle →Notice a new Vector layer was created.*

4.15 Text Layers

Text layers are saved as a vector and can be modified at a later time.

Practice Exercise 40 - Text Layer

1. *File Menu →New → Print Tab →Print Presets →Letter (8.5 x 11 in @ 300 ppi →* Create.
2. *Select the* T *Horizontal Type Tool →Draw a text box →Notice a new Text layer was created.*

4.16 Index Layers

An Index layer is a special layer that can't be modified or unlocked on the **Layers Panel.**

To define an Index Layer: *Image Menu →Mode →* ✔ Indexed Color.

To unlock an Index Layer: *Image Menu →Mode →* ✔ RGB Color *or any mode you desire.*

4.17 Smart Object

Embedded Smart Objects are placed on a special layer that will preserve the original content of an image. You can apply **Photoshop** adjustments such as transforming, resizing, and applying filters. The most important aspect of **Smart Objects** is that they can preserve raster image quality. If a **PSD** file has a lower quality, a **Smart Object** will maintain the original quality. Also, when you scale or rotate a **Smart Object**, the quality will return to the original resolution. An example of using a

Smart Object is to embed **Illustrator** or **Photoshop** files. **To insert a Smart Object:** *File Menu→Place Embedded.*

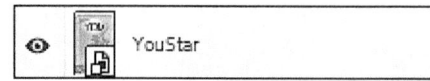

Practice Exercise 41 - Smart Object

File Menu→Place Embedded→C:\Data\PhotoshopCC-2\SmartObjectLabel.psd

4.17-1 Smart Object Linked

This will create a link to an original file. When an original file changes, a **Smart Object** in the **Photoshop** layer will also change. *File→Place Linked.*
To update the image: *Right-Click on the layer→Update modified content.*

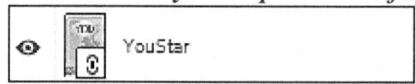

Practice Exercise 42 - Smart Object Linked

File Menu→Place Embedded→YouStar.ill.

4.17-2 Convert Smart Object

You can convert an existing **Layer** to a **Smart Object** and it will function independently as a new **Smart Layer**. *Select the Existing layer→Layer→Smart Objects→Convert to Smart Object.*

4.17-3 Edit Smart Object

This will allow you to edit the characteristics of a **Smart Layer**.
Double click on a Smart Layer or Layer→Smart Objects→Edit Contents.

Practice Exercise 43 - Edit Smart Object

You must have **Illustrator** installed to complete this exercise.
In Photoshop: *Select a layer from the previous practice exercise→Layer→ Smart Objects→Edit Contents.*
In Illustrator: *Change the word "You" to "YYY"→Save and Close Illustrator.*
In Photoshop: *Right-Click on the layer→Update modified content.*
   Or *Right-Click on layer→Relink to file→YouStar.ill.*

4.17-4 Copy Smart Object Layer

This will create another **Smart Object Layer** that will be independent of the original **Smart Layer**: *Layer→Smart Objects→New Smart Object via Copy).*
This may be useful in making cosmetic adjustments to a **Smart Layer**.

4.17-5 Replace Smart Layer Contents

This will update or replace a **Smart Layer**. *Layer Menu→Smart Objects→ Replace Contents→Navigate to the new file→Place.*

4.17-6 Rasterize Smart Object

This will convert a **Smart Layer** to a normal **Photoshop Layer**. *Select the Smart Object layer→Layer→Smart Objects→Rasterize.*

4.17-7 Duplicate Linked Layer

This is used to create another **Smart Object Layer** that is linked to an original file (both will be linked to the same file). It may be useful in making cosmetic adjustments to a **Smart Layer**. *Layer→New→Layer Via Copy or drag the Smart layer to the New Layer Icon* 🔲 You can also copy a **Smart Object Layer**: *Layer→Smart Objects→New Smart Object via Copy).*

Chapter 4 - Advanced Layers

Section 3: Layer Menu

 This is located in the upper right corner of the **Layers Panel.** The following are some of the most commonly used features:

4.18 New Group

This creates a group to organize common layers.

Practice Exercise 44 - Group

Create a **Group** and rename it. Then, drag different **Layers** into the **Group**. You can then collapse or expand the **Group** to reduce clutter.
1. ***File Menu→Open→Sunlight Detergent.psd→*** Open .
2. **Create a Group:** *Select the ≡ More options (located in the upper right corner of the Layers Panel)→New Group→Name: Text Layers.*
3. **Select all text layers using the** Shift **key:** *Select the top layer→Hold the* Shift *key → Select the lower text layer→Drag and drop them on the Group name.*
4. **Collapse/Expand:** *Press the arrow in front of the group name→ Collapse.*

4.19 Link Layer

This will allow you to hook, tie or link **Layers** together. When you move one **Layer,** the others will also move.

4.20 Merge Down

This **Merges** a selected **Layer** and the one beneath it.

4.21 Merge Visible

This **Merges** visible **Layers** when the 👁 Eye is turned on.

Practice Exercise 45 - Merge Visible

Continue from the previous practice exercise.
1. ***Turn off the* 👁 *Eye icon on some Layers.***
2. **Merge Visible:** *Select the ≡ More options (located in the upper right corner of the Layers Panel)→Merge Visible.*
3. ***Only the Visible Layers will be Merged.***

4.22 Flatten Image

This **Flattens** all **Layers** similar to a pancake.

Practice Exercise 46 - Flatten Layers

Continue from the previous practice exercise.
1. **Flatten Layers:** *Select the ≡ More options (located in the upper right corner of the Layers Panel)→Flatten.*
2. ***All layers will be Merged.***

4.23 Panel Options

This will change the size of a **Layer** picture in the **Layers Panel** .
Select the ≡ *More options (located in the upper right corner of the Layers Panel)→Panel options:*

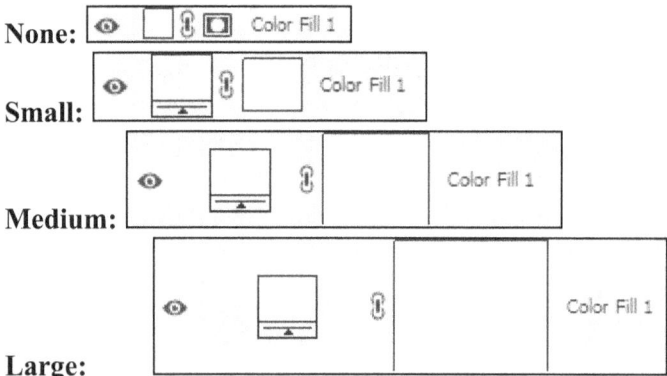

Section 4: Layer Manipulation

These options are listed in the Layer Menu located on top of the Photoshop interface.

4.24 Alignment

This aligns objects placed on different layers: *Create 3 objects on 3 layers →Select all 3 layers → Layer Menu →Align →Vertical Centers.*

4.25 Distribute

This distributes objects placed on different layers: *Create 3 objects on 3 layers →Select all 3 layers → Layer Menu →Distribute →Horizontal Centers.*

4.26 Layer Via Copy

This will create a **New Layer** from a selected object. **Test It:** *Select an object → Layer Menu →New →Layer via Copy.*

4.27 Layer Via Cut

This will create a **New Layer** from a selected object as the original selection disappears. **Test It:** *Select an object → Layer Menu →New →Layer via Cut.*

4.28 Layer

This will create a new blank **Layer**. *Test It: Layer Menu →New →Layer.*

4.29 Duplicate Layer

This will **Duplicate** a selected **Layer**. *Test It: Select a Layer → Layer Menu → Duplicate Layer.*

4.30 Delete Layer

This will **Delete** a selected **Layer**. *Test It: Select an object → Layer Menu → Delete →Layer.*

4.31 Rasterize

This will convert a **Vector Layer** to a **Raster Layer**. For example, when you use the **Type Tool**, a **Vector Layer** is created. Then, this command will **Rasterize** the **Vector Layer**. **Tip**: This can be used to convert a specific font to pixels, no need to maintain a font library. **Test It:** *Type Tool →Draw a Test box →Type some text in the box →Layer Menu → Rasterize.*

Chapter 5 - Image Adjustments

This chapter will focus on **Adjusting Images** on a **Layer**.

Chapter Contents:
Section 1: Canvas and Image Size Adjustment - This will change the size and resolution of an image.
   The concepts include: Image Size, Canvas Size, and Image Compression.
Section 2: Image Adjustments - These tools will primarily change shadows and highlights.
   The concepts include: Auto Tone, Auto Contrast, Auto Color, Brightness/Contrast, Levels, Curves, and Exposure.
Section 3: Color Adjustments - This will adjust colors.
   The concepts include: Vibrance, Hue/Saturation, Color Balance, Black & White, Photo Filter, Channel Mixer, and Color Lookup.
Section 4: Color Replacement Adjustments - This will replace colors rather than drawing colors.
   The concepts include: Invert, Posterize, Threshold, Gradient Map, and Selective Color.
Section 5: Toning Adjustments - These are additional tools to change shadows and highlights.
   The concepts include: Shadows/Highlights and HDR Toning.
Section 6: Other Color Adjustments - These are additional color tools.
   The concepts include: Desaturate, Match Color, Replace Color, and Equalize.

Section 1: Canvas and Image Size Adjustments

This section will allow you to change or convert a high-resolution image to one with a lower resolution. Also, this section will show how a canvas size can be adjusted.

Section Table Of Contents:
5.1 Image Size
5.2 Canvas Size
5.3 Image Compression

5.1 Image Size

An **Image Size** can be adjusted by scaling it up or down and changing the **Resolution**. Oftentimes, **Image Size** refers to the number of **Pixels Per Inch (PPI)** within the image. The more **PPI** the higher the **Resolution** and a low number of **PPI** results in a **Low-Resolution** image. This adjustment can be made at: *Image Menu →Image Size.*

Pixel Dimension - **Pixels** (**Pixel Elements**) look similar to square dots in **Photoshop** when zoomed in extremely close. Each **Pixel** is a different color or shade. The **Resolution** of an image is measured in **PPI** or **Pixels Per Inch** which is the number of **Pixels** in one inch measured vertically and horizontally.

Page Resolution - The overall quality of a picture is measured by its **Resolution**. Normal small size measurement is **72 ppi**, **300 ppi** is an acceptable picture **Resolution** quality, and **1500 ppi** is a very **High-Resolution** picture quality.

You can see from the diagram below that the smaller **Resolution** image is blurry. However, if you were using this image in a zoomed-in state it looks acceptable. When you scale the **72 ppi** image up or make it larger, the resolution doesn't look very clear. But, if you use the **72 ppi** as a small image, such as a logo on a website, it looks just fine.

Chapter 5 - Image Adjustments

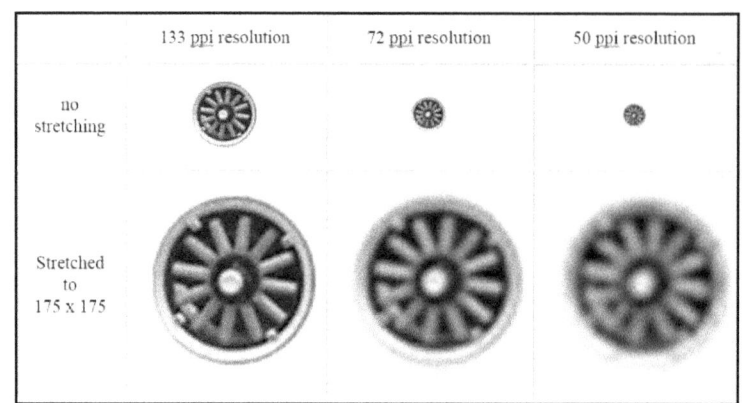

Practice Exercise 47 - Image Resolution

1. **Change an image resolution:**
   File Menu→Open→C:\Data\PhotoshopCC-2\Spice Display.jpg→ Open .
2. **Inspect the file size:** *Image Menu→Image Size→Change inches to Pixels:*

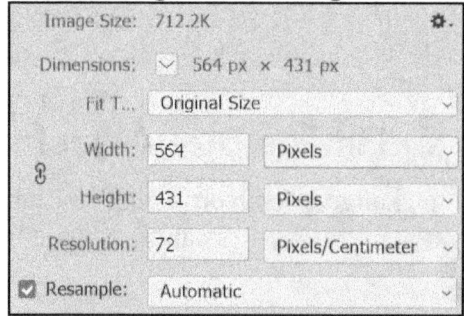

3. *Reduce the file size by changing the image size pixel dimension to 320x240 pixels.*

   Image Size: 225.0K
   Dimensions: 320 px × 240 px

5.2 Canvas Size

A **Canvas** is the base size of a background or frame. This defines the dimensions of the frame such as 8-1/2 X 11, 7x5in, 5x7in, 10x10in, etc. If you intend to print a picture in a 7x5in frame, then you must define the **Canvas** area as 7x5in. If you reduce the **Canvas** size in an existing image, you might end up chopping the picture. It is best to define a blank **Canvas** and then move the image to the new **Canvas**. At that point, you can scale or change the size of the image to fit the **Canvas**.

Document Size - The size of the **Pixels Per Inch (PPI)** number will increase or decrease depending on the size of a **Canvas** area or frame. For example, a regular 7x5 **Canvas** with a high-resolution image (300ppi) will result in a large file size. A regular 7x5 **Canvas** with a low-resolution image (100ppi) will result in a smaller file size because there are fewer **Pixels Per Inch**.

Practice Exercise 48 - Canvas1

1. *File Menu→Open→C:\Data\PhotoshopCC-2\Maestro.jpg→* Open .
2. **Create a Blank Canvas:** *File Menu→New→Photo Tab→Select* `7 x 5 in @ 300 ppi` *→Change the following parameters:*

Chapter 5 - Image Adjustments

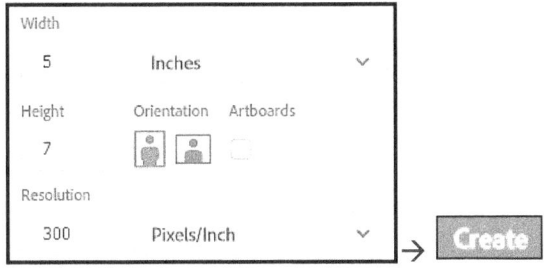

3. **Rearrange Windows Side-By-Side:** *Window Menu→Arrange→ Tile All Vertically.*
4. **Move Picture to an empty Canvas:** ✥ *Move Tool→Select Maestro Picture→Move to the blank Canvas.*
5. **Transform Layer1:** *Select Picture Layer (not the blank Canvas)→Edit Menu→Free Transform→Fit the image in the new Canvas.*
   Tip: You may lose part of a picture in order to fit it on a new **Canvas**.

Practice Exercise 49 - Canvas2

1. *File Menu→Open→C:\Data\PhotoshopCC-2\Beatles.jpg→* Open .
2. **Create a Blank Canvas:** *File Menu→New→Photo Tab→Select* 7 x 5 in @ 300 ppi *→Change the following parameters:*

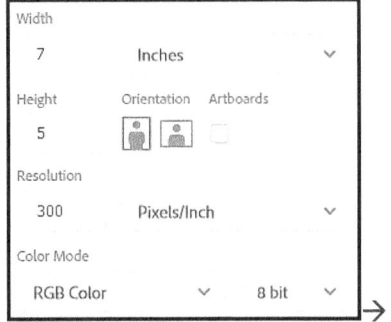

3. **Rearrange Windows Side-By-Side:** *Window Menu→Arrange→ Tile All Vertically.*
4. **Move Picture to an empty Canvas:** ✥ *Move Tool→Select Beatles Picture→Move to the blank Canvas.*
5. **Transform Layer1:** *Select Picture Layer (not the blank Canvas)→Edit Menu→Free Transform→Fit the image in the new Canvas.*
   Tip: You may lose part of a picture in order to fit it on the new **Canvas**.

Chapter 5 - Image Adjustments

5.3 Image Compression

You can **Compress** an **Image** by using the **Image Size** option (*Image Menu→Image Size*). When the ☑ **Resample** checkbox is checked, the **Image** resolution will be adjusted up (**Upsample**) or down (**Downsample**) based on desired adjustment.

To **Downsample** an image, check the "☑ **Resample**" checkbox, choose a **Downsampling** technique in the **Image Compression** area, and then enter a lower resolution.

To **Upsample** check the "☑ **Resample**," choose an Image compression technique, and enter a higher resolution. **Upsampling,** will increase the number of pixels or make an image larger.

Tip: One technique is to increase (**Upsample**) in small increments and view results filling smaller areas multiple times. This will increase the **Upsample** and will result in better quality.

The following will describe the sophisticated adjustment technique available:
Image Menu →Image Size→ ☑ *Resample Image→Choose one of the following:*
   Nearest Neighbor - This is used to resize illustrations, but it can create jagged edges.
   Bilinear - This gives an average result by balancing speed and quality based on image pixels.
   Bicubic - This is the best method used to resample an image. It is a slow-paced method but produces a more precise effect.
   Bicubic Smoother - This is an improved bicubic method designed to enlarge images or **Upsampling**.
   Bicubic Sharper - This is an improved bicubic method designed to reduce the size of images or **Downsampling**.

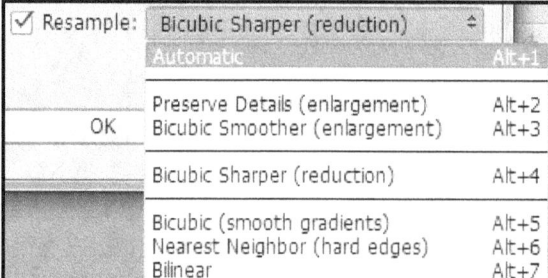

Tip: You can test or sample each one above to view the result. However, the **Automatic** option will choose the best option for an image being **Downsampled**.

Practice Exercise 50 - Bicubic

There is a very subtle difference between different **Resamples**.
1. *File Menu→Open→C:\Data\PhotoshopCC-2\Maestro.jpg→* Open .
2. *Zoom In to her eye→Image Menu→Image Size→Resolution: 50→* ☑ **Resample:** *Bicubic Sharper.*

Chapter 5 - Image Adjustments

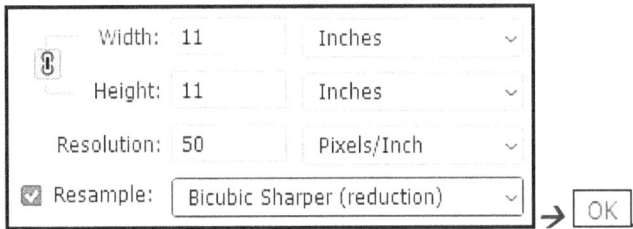

3. *Zoom In to the eye to see differences.*

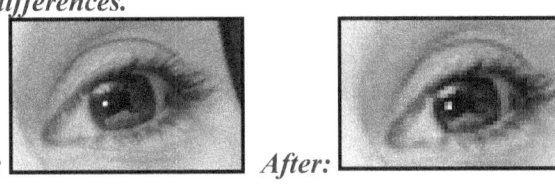

Before: *After:*

Section 2: Image Adjustments

There are two ways to adjust an image but this section will focus on **Layer Destructive Adjustments.**

Destructive Image Adjustments

   This feature allows you to **Adjust** the tone of an image on a **Layer** and will permanently change it.

   Tip: In order to protect the original **Layer**, make several copies of it in case an error occurs. Apply the **Adjustment** to a **Layer** located on top of the **Layers Panel**.

1. *Right-click on Layer to be duplicated→Duplicate Layer.*
2. *Select the top Layer.*
3. *Image Menu→Adjustments→Choose the desired Adjustment option.*

Non-Destructive Image Adjustments

   This will create a new **Adjustment Layer** on top while all **Layers** beneath will show effects of the adjustments. Think of this as a special glass cover that you can see through, or a filter that disguises the lower **Layers**. This film can be removed at a later time by dragging the filter (next to the **Layer**) to the 🗑 **Trash Can** (located in the lower right corner of the **Layers Panel**), if necessary. It makes the **Adjustment Non-Destructive** because the particular **Adjustment** can be removed.

   Layer Panel→Right-click on a layer→Choose Duplicate→Select a Layer →Adjustment Layer ⬤ *(located on the bottom of the Layer Panel) or use the **Adjustments Panel**: Window→Adjustments.*

Section Table Of Contents:

   5.4 Auto Tone
   5.5 Auto Contrast
   5.6 Auto Color
   5.7 Brightness/Contrast
   5.8 Levels
   5.9 Curves
   5.10 Exposure

Practice Exercise 51 - Destructive vs Non-Destructive

   This will demonstrate the two techniques.

1. *File Menu→Open→C:\Data\PhotoshopCC-2\Browies.png→* Open .
2. **Method 1: Destructive Adjustment Layer:**
   2a. *Right-Click on the desired layer→Duplicate Layer.*
   2b. Select the Image Adjustments: *Image Menu→Adjustments→ Brightness/Contrast→(change settings).*
3. **Method 2: Non-Destructive** ⬤ **Fill or Adjustment Layer:**

Chapter 5 - Image Adjustments

3a. *Select the main layer→Create Fill or Adjustment Layer (located on the bottom of the Layers Panel) →(change the brightness level).*
3b. *The layers will look similar to the following:*

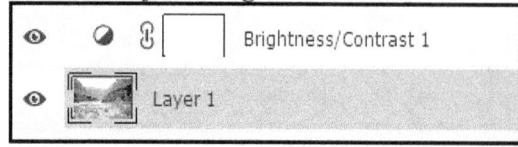

5.4 Auto Tone

This will adjust the dark pixels to black and lighter pixels to white. It then redistributes the center point. **Auto Tone** works best for average images with even intensity of highlights (bright areas), shadows (dark areas), and mid-tones. *Image Menu→Auto Tone.*

5.5 Auto Contrast

This removes the lightest and darkest pixels and then makes highlights brighter and shadows darker. *Image Menu→Auto Contrast.*

5.6 Auto Color

This neutralizes the darkest and lightest pixels. It does a good job of correcting many images which are improperly exposed. *Image Menu→Auto Color.*

Practice Exercise 52 - Auto Tone, Contrast, Color

1. *File Menu→Open→C:\Data\PhotoshopCC-2\Daniel Carina.jpg→* Open .
2. *Make three copies: Right-click on a Layer→Duplicate or drag the Layer to the ⊞ New Layer Icon.*
3. *Select the Top Layer→Image Menu→Auto Tone→Review the results.*
4. *Turn off the ⊙ Eye on the top layer.*
5. *Select the next layer down→Image Menu→Auto Contrast→Review the results.*
6. *Turn off the ⊙ Eye on that Layer.*
7. *Select the next Layer down→Image Menu→Auto Color→Review the results.*
8. *Turn the Eye off on several Layers to see differences.*

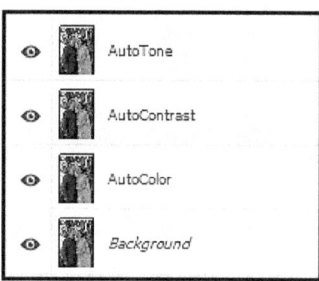

5.7 Brightness/Contrast

This is one of the most commonly used commands to lighten or darken an overall image. **Contrast** will lighten shadows and darken highlights. However, it will also discard valuable tonal information from all images.
Window Panel→Histogram, Image Menu →Adjustments→ Brightness/Contrast.

Chapter 5 - Image Adjustments

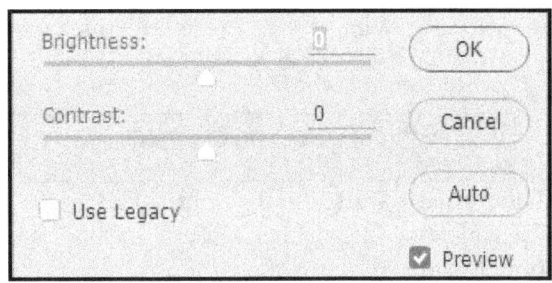

Practice Exercise 53 - Brightness/Contrast

Undo the previous practice exercise by pressing Undo or Ctrl Z.
File Menu →Open →C:\Data\PhotoshopCC-2\Daniel Carina.jpg→ Open .
Image Menu →Adjustments →Brightness/Contrast.

5.8 Levels

This uses a **Histogram** to display how dark and light pixels are concentrated together. The following are a few options to consider:

Eye Dropper - This is used to sample dark points, mid-points, and white points. **Eye Dropper** will highlight a specific color across an entire image. **Test It:** Select the white points icon in **Levels**, then select a white or lighter point on a document.

Auto - This can sometimes do an acceptable job on neutral colors and can also adjust an image for color balance and exposure issues. However, it is greatly enhanced in CS6.

Tip: The following example was based on: *File Menu →Open →*
C:\Data\PhotoshopCC-2\Daniel Carina.jpg→ Open *→Image Menu →Adjustments →Layers*.

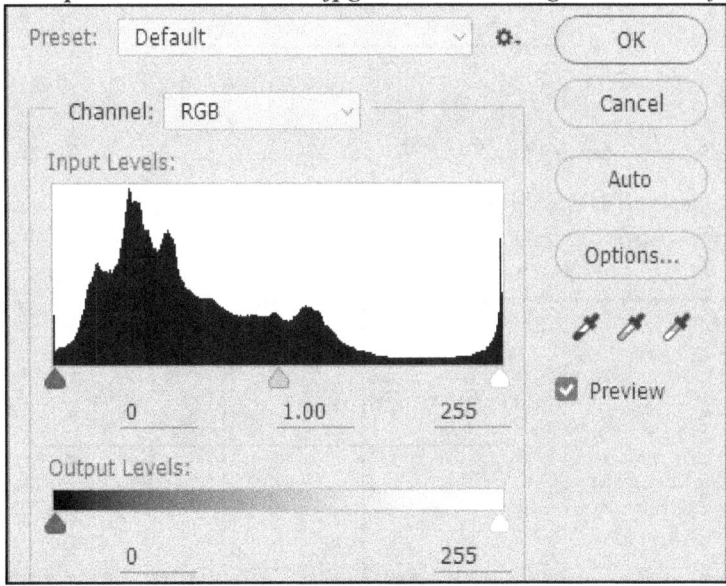

Dark Pixels - This is a concentration of **Dark Pixels** or shadows that could indicate the image has been underexposed.

Light Pixels - This is a concentration of **Light Pixels** or highlights which indicates overexposure.

Center Point - This is the middle of a pixel cluster.

Chapter 5 - Image Adjustments

The dark pixels in the **Histogram** above are shifted to the left which means there is an underexposed darker image to repair. To fix it, slide the white triangle on the left to the beginning of the dark pixel clusters to the left. See Below:

If the dark pixels in the **Histogram** are shifted to the right, then there is an over-exposed mage. In order to repair this type of **Histogram**, drag the black triangle to the right. Then, adjust the center slider in order to get the correct shade. See below:

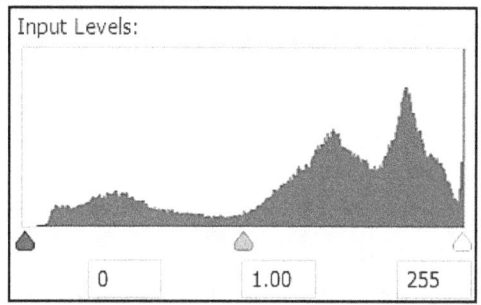

Test It: *Press* Options... *button →Select ○ Enhance Per Channel Contrast and ☑ Snap Neutral Midtones to see the results.*

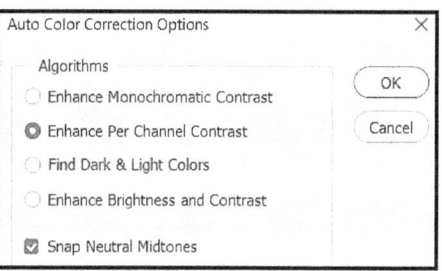

Practice Exercise 54 - Levels Underexposed

1. ***File Menu→Open→C:\Data\PhotoshopCC-2\Car Hood.jpg→*** Open .
2. ***Image Menu→Adjustment→Levels.***
3. ***To repair the image move the white triangle to the left and adjust the gray (middle) triangle.***

Original: [Input Levels: 0, 1.00, 255] Adjusted: [Input Levels: 0, 1.5, 102]

4. ***Review the Image results.***

Practice Exercise 55 - Levels

1. ***File Menu→Open→C:\Data\PhotoshopCC-2\Convertible.jpg→*** Open .
2. ***Image Menu→Adjustment→Levels.***
3. ***To repair the image by moving the white and dark triangle. Also, adjust the gray triangle.***

Chapter 5 - Image Adjustments

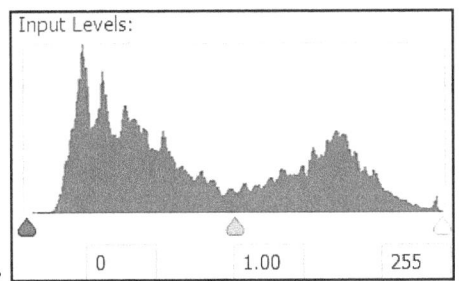 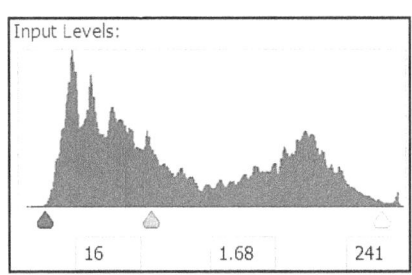

Original: *Adjusted:*

4. *Review the image results.*

Practice Exercise 56 - Levels Overexposed

1. ***File Menu→Open→C:\Data\PhotoshopCC-2\Sea Cliff.jpg→*** Open .
2. ***Image Menu→Adjustment→Levels.***
3. ***To repair the image by moving the white and dark triangle. Also, adjust the gray triangle.***

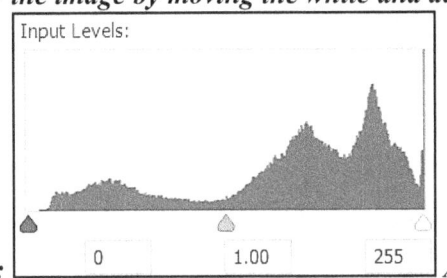 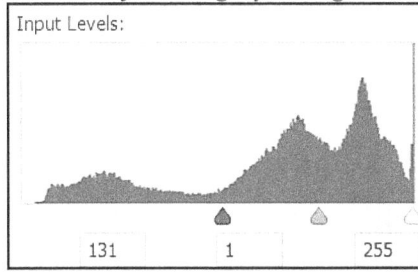

Original: *Adjusted:*

4. *Review the image results.*

5.9 Curves

This is used to darken/lighten a specific color within an image. It provides up to 16 control points and the strength of individual colors can be controlled. The left side of the **Curve** controls and eliminates **RGB** highlights which will make an image light. The bottom edge controls will eliminate **RGB** shadows which will make an image darker. **Tip:** If an image has been saved as a **CMYK** color, the controls will be the opposite.

Auto - This option will attempt to repair an image. ***Options Panel→X Auto options***

Black Eye Dropper 🖋 - This blows up shadows of an image.

Middle Eye Dropper 🖋 - This is used for setting neutral gray.

White Eye Dropper 🖋 - This blows up highlights of an image.

Chapter 5 - Image Adjustments

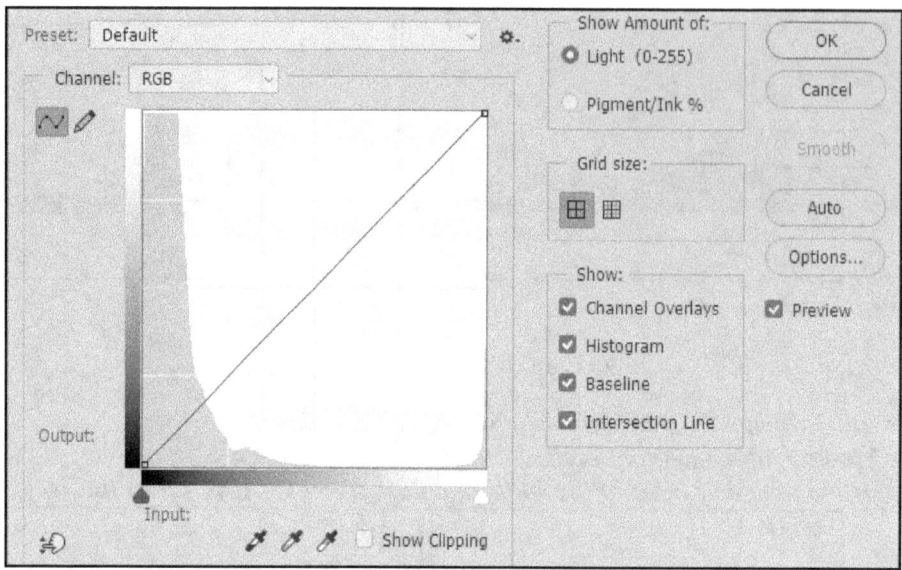

Practice Exercise 57 - Open File Family.jpg

File Menu →Open →C:\Data\PhotoshopCC-2\Family.jpg→ Open .
Image Menu → Adjustments → Curves.
Test It: Test the controls by moving the line.

5.10 Exposure

This **Re-exposes** an image if it is **Under-exposed** or **Over-exposed**. When a camera's shutter is open too long, an image becomes **Over-exposed**. **Under-exposure** happens when a camera's shutter is open for a short amount of time.

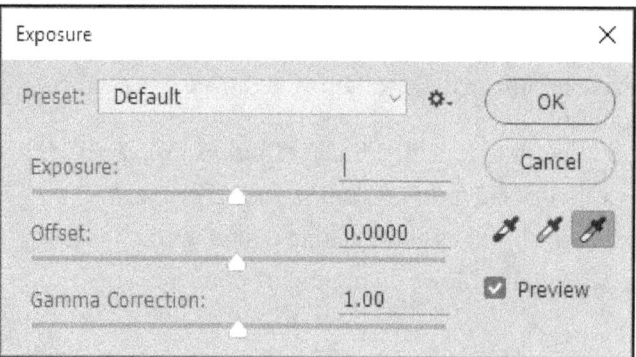

Practice Exercise 58 - Exposure

File Menu →Open →C:\Data\PhotoshopCC-2\SurferWoman.jpg→ Open .
Image Menu → Adjustments →Exposure.

Section 3: Color Adjustments

This section will focus on **Adjustments** that apply **Color** to an image.

Section Table Of Contents:
   5.11 Vibrance
   5.12 Hue/Saturation
   5.13 Color Balance

Chapter 5 - Image Adjustments

5.14 Black & White
5.15 Photo Filter
5.16 Channel Mixer
5.17 Color Lookup.

5.11 Vibrance

Vibrance boosts only those parts of a photo that are less saturated. It also respects skin tones, which means photos look more natural when pumping up the intensity of color.

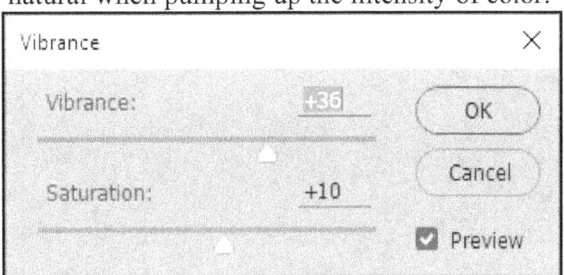

Practice Exercise 59 - Vibrance

File Menu →Open →C:\Data\PhotoshopCC-2\Face Wrinkles.jpg → Open .
Image Menu → Adjustments →Vibrance.

5.12 Hue/Saturation

This is primarily used to saturate a picture with a specific color or adjust the overall color intensity. For example, when you saturate a yellow flower with red, the flower turns completely red. *Image Menu → Adjustments →Hue/Saturation or Layer Menu →New Adjustment Layer →Hue/Saturation.*

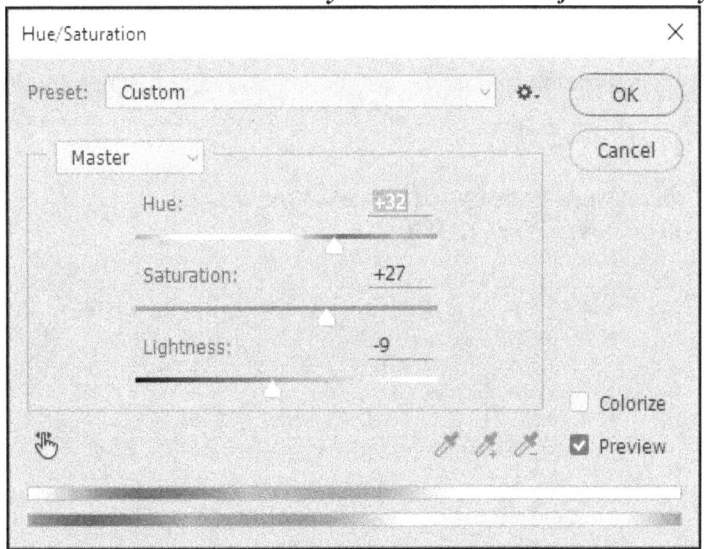

Practice Exercise 60 - Hue/Saturation

File Menu →Open →C:\Data\PhotoshopCC-2\Landscape.jpg → Open .
Image Menu →Adjustments →Hue/Saturation →Move the sliders to adjust colors.

5.13 Color Balance

This is very helpful in order to change color tone or add more color overall to an image. For skin tone that is not an actual flesh color, you can add red to bring out natural color. Some images may never need a color shade added to provide a more realistic look.

Duplicate the background Image (Ctrl J) → fx →Blending options→General Blending→Blend Mode: Multiply, Image Menu→ Adjustments→ Color balance (Make blue more yellow +20 +54 -64).

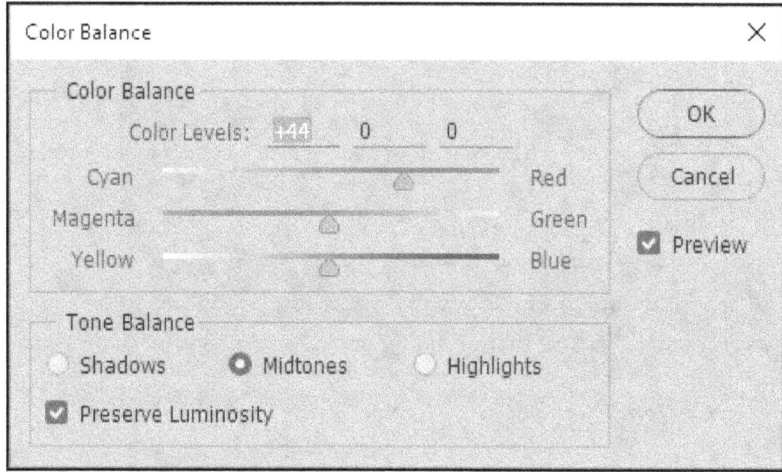

Practice Exercise 61 - Color Balance

File Menu→Open→C:\Data\PhotoshopCC-2\Maestro.jpg→ Open .
Image Menu→ Adjustments→ Color Balance →Adjust the red tones.

5.14 Black & White

Color sliders adjust the saturation of specific colors to a converted **Black** and **White** image.

Practice Exercise 62 - Black & White

File Menu→Open→C:\Data\PhotoshopCC-2\Twins.jpg→ Open .
Image Menu→ Adjustments→Black & White.

Chapter 5 - Image Adjustments

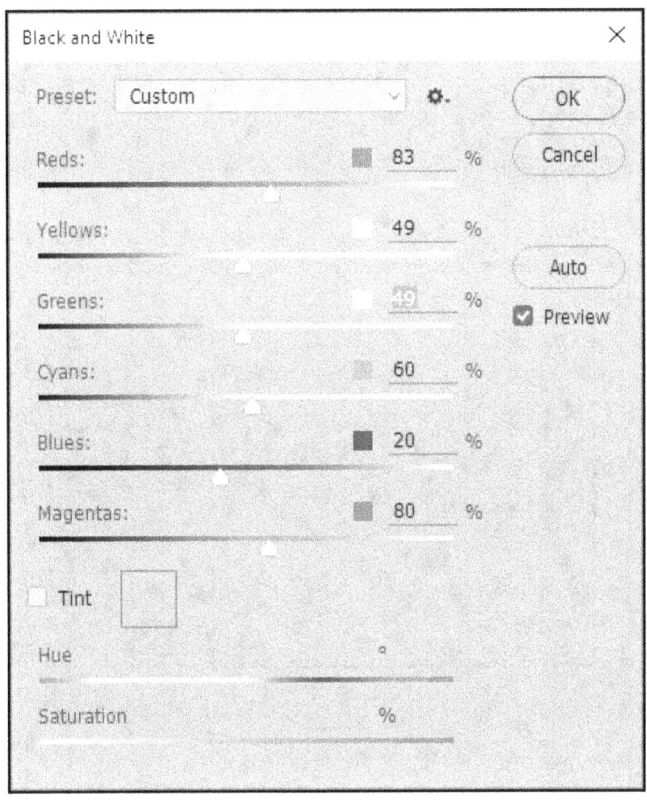

5.15 Photo Filter

This places a color **Photo Filter** over a black and white picture in order to change the look of an image. One common technique is to apply a brownish shade (Sepia) to a black and white image.

Practice Exercise 63 - Photo Filter

File Menu →Open →C:\Data\PhotoshopCC-2\Tony's First Communion.jpg→ Open *.*
→Image Menu → Mode → RGB → Image Menu → Adjustments →Photo Filter → Filter: Sepia→Density: 100%.

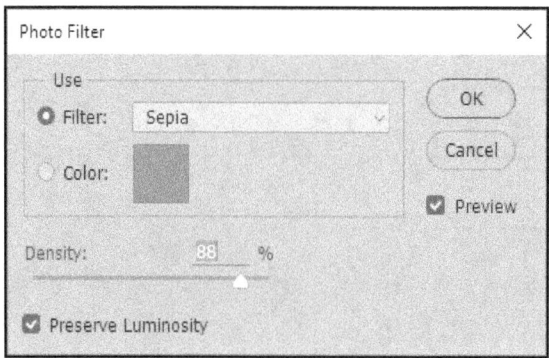

5.16 Channel Mixer

Colors are defined in channels such as **RGB** (**Red**, **Green**, **Blue**). This technique allows you to mix or cross over defined channels.

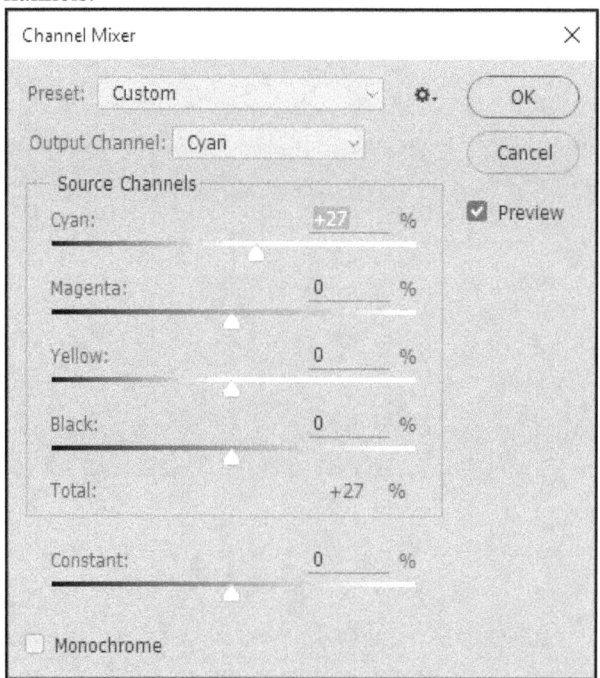

Practice Exercise 64 - Channel Mixer

File Menu →Open →C:\Data\PhotoshopCC-2\Cafe.jpg→ Open *.*
Image Menu → Adjustments →Channel Mixer →Make adjustments.

Chapter 5 - Image Adjustments

5.17 Color Lookup

This allows you to instantly change the overall appearance of a photo by simply choosing from three defined presets.

Practice Exercise 65 - Color Lookup

File Menu →Open →C:\Data\PhotoshopCC-2\Maestro.jpg→ Open .

Image Menu → Adjustments →Color Lookup → 3DLUT File Load 3D LUT... .
Tip: Try **FallColors.look**, **DropBlues.3DL**, or **Crisp_Warm.look**.

Section 4: Color Replacement Adjustment

Section Table Of Contents:
5.18 Invert
5.19 Posterize
5.20 Threshold
5.21 Gradient Map
5.22 Selective Color

5.18 Invert

This **Inverts** the color spectrum to an opposite color.

Practice Exercise 66 - Invert

File Menu →Open →C:\Data\PhotoshopCC-2\Art Cube.png→ Open .
Image Menu → Adjustments →Invert.

5.19 Posterize

The **Posterize** adjustment allows you to specify the number of tonal levels (or brightness values) for each channel in an image. Then, it maps pixels to the closest matching level. This can produce interesting effects.

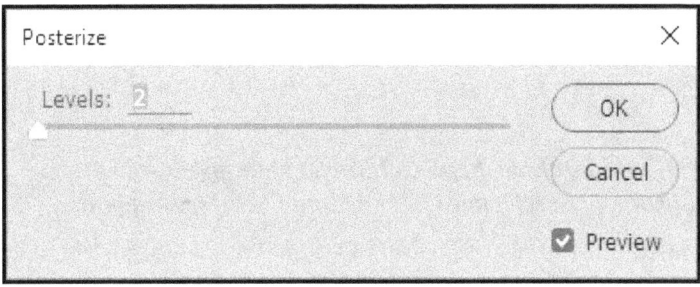

Page 69

Chapter 5 - Image Adjustments

Practice Exercise 67 - Posterize

File Menu →Open →C:\Data\PhotoshopCC-2\Beatles.jpg→ Open .
Image Menu → Adjustments → Posterize.

5.20 Threshold

This converts an image to black and white and separates a color from its original spectrum.

Practice Exercise 68 - Threshold

File Menu →Open →C:\Data\PhotoshopCC-2\Convertible.jpg→ Open .
Image Menu → Adjustments → Move the slider on the bottom to get the desired effect.

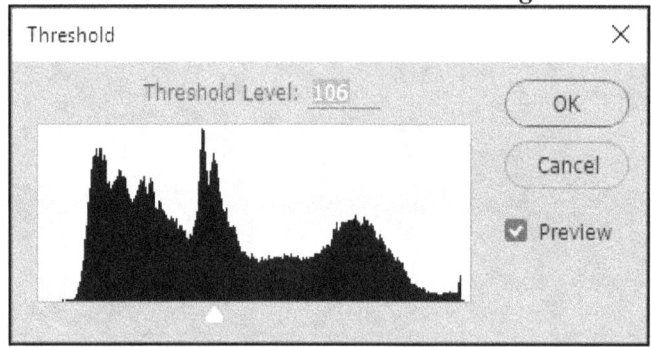

5.21 Gradient Map

This converts an image to grayscale and then replaces a range of black, gray, and white tones with a choice of gradient. In effect, it colorizes the image.

Practice Exercise 69 - Gradient map

File Menu →Open →C:\Data\PhotoshopCC-2\Landscape.jpg→ Open .
Image Menu → Adjustments → Gradient Map.

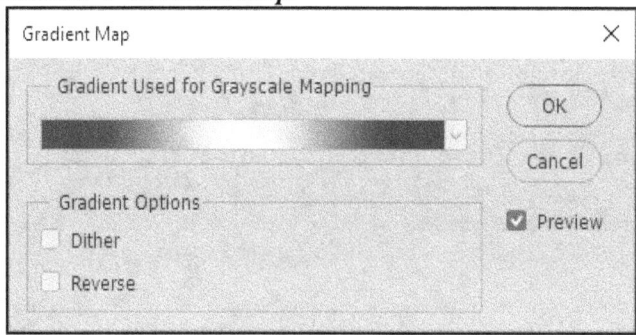

5.22 Selective Color

This provides a somewhat limited, but useful, ability to independently adjust one color inside another color.

Practice Exercise 70 - Selective Color

File Menu →Open →C:\Data\PhotoshopCC-2\SurferMan.jpg→ Open .
Image Menu → Adjustments →Selective Color→Color: Blues→Magenta: -78

Chapter 5 - Image Adjustments

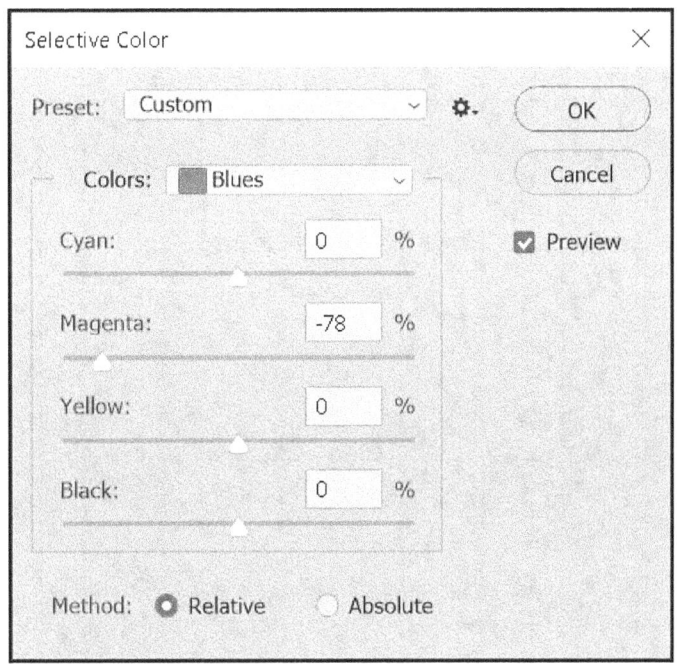

Section 5: Toning Adjustments

Section Table Of Contents:
    5.23 Shadows/Highlights
    5.24 HDR Toning

5.23 Shadows/Highlights

Changing **Shadows** (darker areas) and **Highlights** (lighter areas) can directly affect pixels. Be sure to copy a layer before making this adjustment. This will simply lighten or darken all shadows and highlights.

Practice Exercise 71 - Shadows/Highlights

1. *File Menu→Open →C:\Data\PhotoshopCC-2\Sea Cliff.jpg→* `Open`
2. *Layer Panel→Right Click on the background layer→Duplicate Layer*
3. *Image Menu → Adjustments → Shadow/Highlights →Change the Amount to 33%.*

Chapter 5 - Image Adjustments

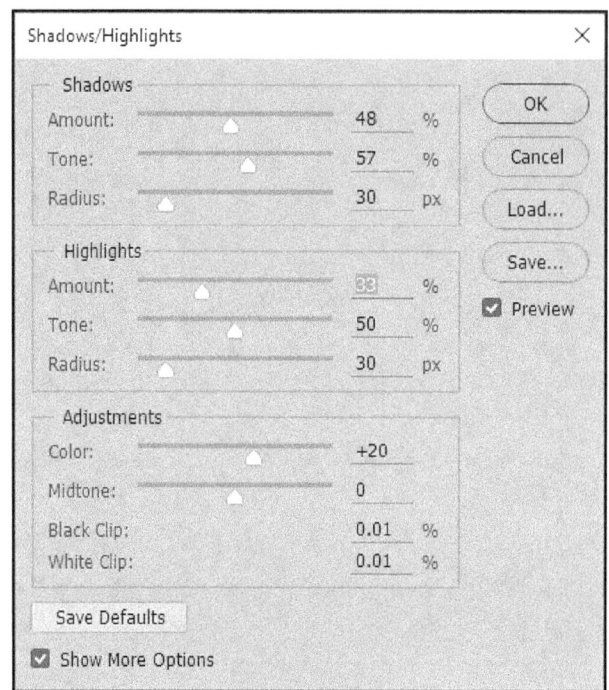

4. *Turn on/off the ⊙ Eye icon in Layer 1 to compare the difference:*
5. **Test It:** Test these features using the file **Red-eye.jpg**.

5.24 HDR Toning

HDR (High Dynamic Range) toning flattens colors for edges, exposures, shadows, highlights, vibrance, and saturation. It also enhances images with dark shadows.

Practice Exercise 72 - HDR Toning

1. *File Menu→Open→C:\Data\PhotoshopCC-2\Canoe Boy.jpg→* Open .
2. *Image Menu→Adjustments→HDR Toning.*
3. *Try changing the Strength, Exposure, Shadow, and Highlight parameters.*

Chapter 5 - Image Adjustments

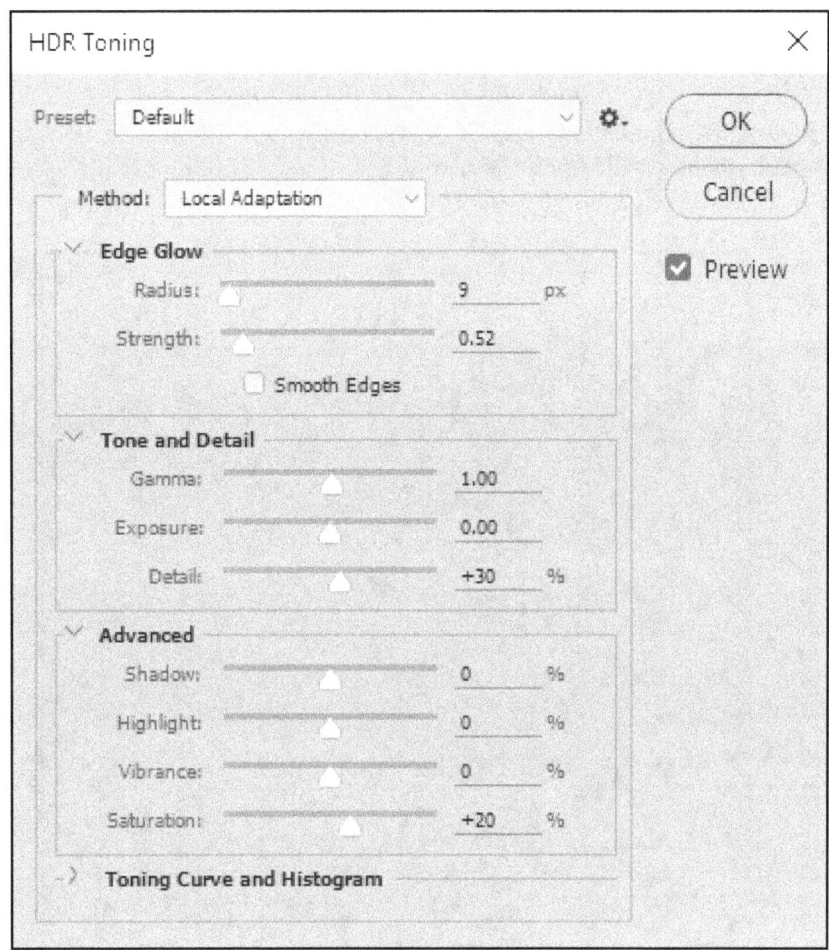

4. **Test It:** Test these features using the file **Car Hood.jpg**.

Section 6: Other Color Adjustments

Section Table Of Contents:
5.25 Desaturate
5.26 Match Color
5.27 Replace Color
5.28 Equalize

5.25 Desaturate

The image will look like a black and white photo.

Practice Exercise 73 - Desaturate

File Menu →Open →C:\Data\PhotoshopCC-2\Kids.gif → Open .
Image Menu →Adjustments → Desaturate.

5.26 Match Color

This matches colors from a different image. Here, you can switch to different secondary images in order to see new effects.

Chapter 5 - Image Adjustments

Practice Exercise 74 - Match Color

> *File Menu →Open →C:\Data\PhotoshopCC-2\Countryside.jpg→* Open .
> *File Menu →Open →C:\Data\PhotoshopCC-2\Harbor.jpg→* Open .
> *Image Menu →Adjustments →Match Color →*
> *Image Statistics/Source → Choose a different source such as Countryside.jpg to view the differences.*

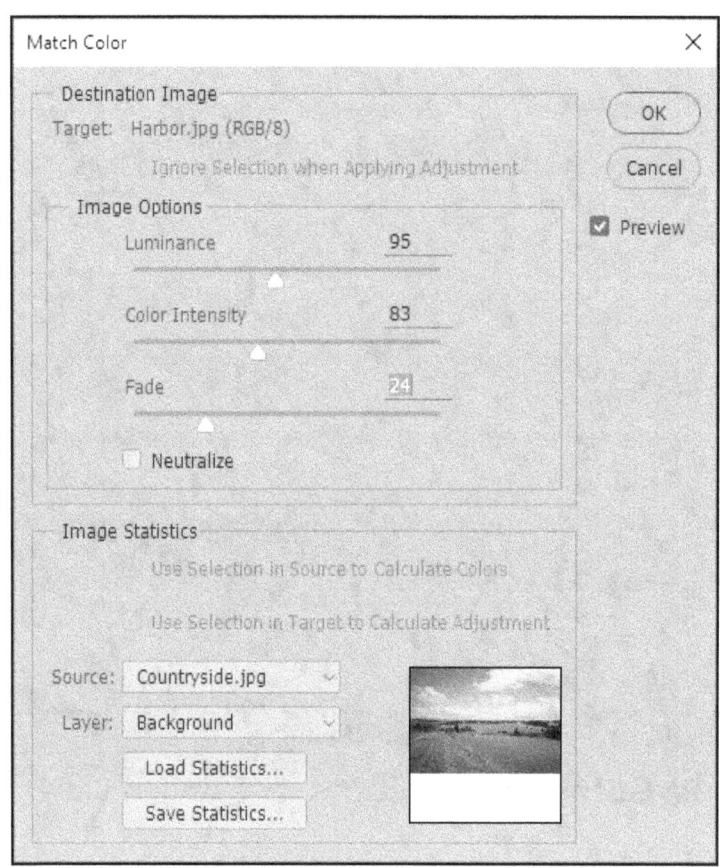

5.27 Replace Color

This allows you to sample an image using the **Eyedropper Tool** (top of the dialog box), and then replace the color with a different one (lower portion of the dialog box).

Practice Exercise 75 - Replace Color

> *File Menu →Open →C:\Data\PhotoshopCC-2\Landscape.jpg→* Open .
> *Image Menu →Adjustments →Replace Color →Sample the sky using the Eyedropper Tool.*
>> *Make sure the Eye Dropper is selected*
>> *Ensure the entire image is affected* .
>> *Sample the grass with the eyedropper.*
>> *Adjust the following to replace the color.*
>>> **When finished, choose** OK .

Test It: Try sampling the sidewalk area and replacing the **Hue**, **Saturation**, and **Lightness**.

Chapter 5 - Image Adjustments

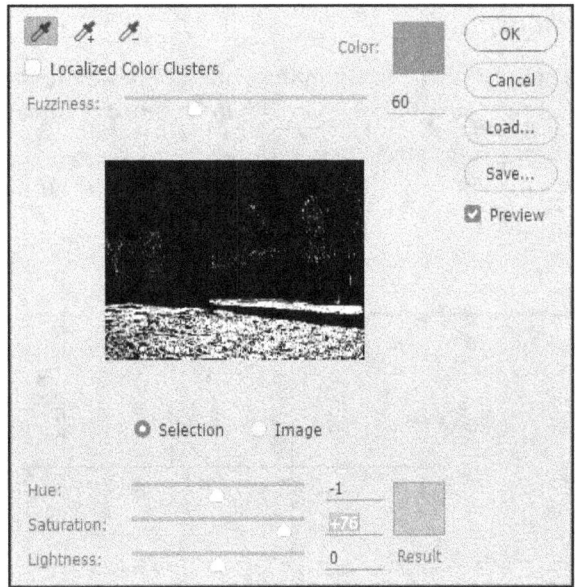

5.28 Equalize

This redistributes the brightness values in an image so that the overall range is more evenly represented.

Practice Exercise 76 - Equalize

File Menu → Open → C:\Data\PhotoshopCC-2\Country.jpg → Open.
Image Menu → Adjustments → Equalize. **Tip:** *Also, try Harbor.jpg.*

Chapter 5 - Image Adjustments

Student Project C - Adjustments

Step 1: Open the image indicated below (located in the *C:\Data\PhotoshopCC-2* **folder**).

Step 2: Make several copies of the background layer ***Window Menu → Layer Menu → Select Background Layer → Drag it to the Create New Layer icon***.

Step 3: The numbers indicate an order for adjusting layers. Rename the numbers to monitor changes.

Step 4: Turn layers on and off to view the differences.

Problem With Image	Example Files	Levels	Levels (eye dropper)	Autolevel	Auto Contrast	Autocolor	Curves	Curves (eye dropper)	Color Balance	Brightness/ Contrast	Hue/Saturation	Desaturate	Match Color	Replace Color	Selective Color
Brightens up a specified color:	Canoe Boy.jpg	3	4					1		2					
Brightens up dark areas:	Mountain Trail.jpg, Harbor.jpg	3					4		1	2					
Darkens a very light photo:	Sea Cliff.jpg	3					4		2	1					
Fix faded old pictures:	Old Picture1.png Old Picture2.jpg	1		2	3	4	5	6	7	8	9				
Change the color intensity:	Two Flowers.jpg										1				
Dull Picture:	Ancestors.jpg		1				2								
Brightens-Up flowers:	Flowering Branch.jpg		1							2					
Color: Green, Adjust color:	Green Girls.jpg												3	2	1
Replace Shirt color:	Allie Zach.jpg													1	

Chapter 6 - Masking Capabilities

Masking is a cutout technique that conceals or reveals different elements contained in a layer. It is similar to a Halloween mask on a person's face, when the eyes are cut out it reveals the eyes of a person but conceals the rest of their face. In this chapter, we will cover many different types of **Layer Mask** techniques available.

Chapter Contents:
Section 1: Select And Mask - This opens a **Panel** in order to fine-tune a selection.
    The concepts include: Select and Mask Button, Drawing Adjustment Tools, Background Overlays, View Mode, Refine Mode, Edge Detection, Global Refinement, and Output Settings.
Section 2: Quick Mask - This is a technique for fine-tuning selected areas.
    The concepts include: Quick Mask Painting and Quick Mask Background Color,
Section 3: Layer Masks - This is a way to place a mask or film on top of a layer to display its specific parts.
    The concepts include Reveal Selection, Hide Selection, and Replace Sky.
Section 4: Clipping Mask - This is a way to clip core information and view a background through that clip.
    The concept include: Clipping Mask.
Section 5: Advanced Techniques - This remembers specific objects that can be moved or adjusted.
    The concepts include: Content-Aware Scale, Content-Aware Move Tool, Content-Aware Fill, and Puppet Warp Tool.

Section 1: Select and Mask

Section Table Of Contents:
    6.1 Select and Mask Button
    6.2 Drawing Adjustment Tools
    6.3 Background Overlays
    6.4 View Mode
    6.5 Refine Mode
    6.6 Edge Detection
    6.7 Global Refinement
    6.8 Output Settings.

6.1 Select and Mask Button

This is used to finetune or adjust an edge of a particular selection in order to increase, decrease, or adjust the edge and fade it out into the background. You will need to rename the **Background Layer** in the **Layers Panel** by double-clicking on the **Background Layer** and then renaming it. **Tip**: In previous versions, this feature was called **Refine Edge**. (*Select an area→Select Menu→Select and Mask*).

6.2 Drawing Adjustment Tools

The following are **Drawing Tools** located in the upper left-hand corner of the **Select and Mask** options. These are used to adjust an edge of a selected area:

Quick Selection Tool - This will select an area based on colors and textures. A selection will then cling to the border of an object.

Refine Edge Brush Tool - This will fine-tune the edge of a selected area.

Brush Tool - This will allow you to add or remove parts of the selected areas. To remove a selection, hold the Alt key down as you draw using the **Brush Tool**.

Chapter 6 - Masking Capabilities

Object Selection Tool - This is used to select objects. It uses **Artificial Intelligence (AI)** programs to find the main object in a picture. When you click on the object, the program will begin analyzing to identify the main image and select it.

Lasso Tool - This draws a freehand selection around a shape. You can then return to the beginning point to complete the selection.

Hand Tool - This is a **Neutral Tool** and will move a canvas when you are zoomed in.

Zoom Tool - After an initial selection, **Zoom In** to see the flaws. **Tip**: Use the **Alt** key to **Zoom out**

6.3 Background Overlays

The following are ways to view a selected image and observe the changes.

Select an area → Select Menu → Select and Mask → View Mode 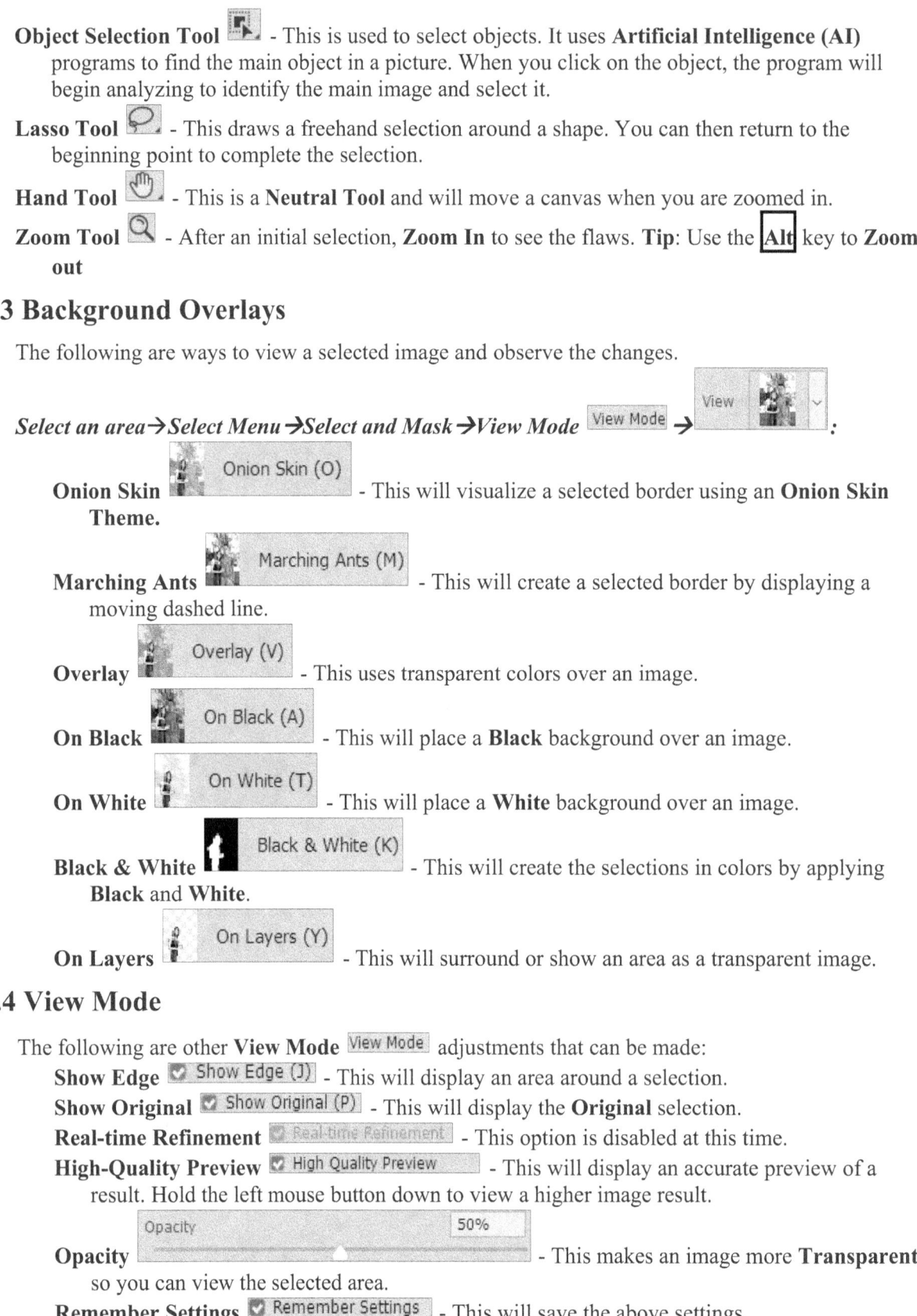 :

Onion Skin - This will visualize a selected border using an **Onion Skin Theme.**

Marching Ants - This will create a selected border by displaying a moving dashed line.

Overlay - This uses transparent colors over an image.

On Black - This will place a **Black** background over an image.

On White - This will place a **White** background over an image.

Black & White - This will create the selections in colors by applying **Black** and **White**.

On Layers - This will surround or show an area as a transparent image.

6.4 View Mode

The following are other **View Mode** adjustments that can be made:

Show Edge - This will display an area around a selection.

Show Original - This will display the **Original** selection.

Real-time Refinement - This option is disabled at this time.

High-Quality Preview - This will display an accurate preview of a result. Hold the left mouse button down to view a higher image result.

Opacity - This makes an image more **Transparent** so you can view the selected area.

Remember Settings - This will save the above settings.

Chapter 6 - Masking Capabilities

6.5 Refine Mode

The following are **Refine Mode** adjustments that can be made:

Color Aware - This will focus on the contrast of background and foreground objects.

Object Aware - This is used for refining hair on complex backgrounds.

6.6 Edge Detection

The following are **Edge Detection** adjustments made to a selection:

- This determines the size of a selected border. Use a small radius to display sharp **Edges** and a large radius for softer or smoother ones.

Smart Radius - This allows a variable width refinement around an edge of a selected area.

6.7 Global Refinement

The following are **Global Refinement** adjustments:

Smooth - This reduces irregular areas and creates a **Smoother** border edge.

Feather - This will blur an edge between a selection edge and the surrounding area.

Contrast - This will create a softer edge transition along a selection border.

Shift Edge - This will move a soft edge border inward (towards 0%) or outward (towards 100%).

6.8 Output Settings

The following are **Output Settings**:

Decontaminate - This will replace edges with nearby pixels.

Amount - This will move the overall selection outward (towards 100%) and inward (towards 0%).

Output To - These are different ways to save results of the options above: 1) **Selection**, 2) **Layer Mask**, 3) **New Layer**, 4) **New Layer with Layer Mask**, 5) **New Document**, or 6) **New Document with Layer Mask**.

Reset the Workspace - This will revert a setting to its original state.

Chapter 6 - Masking Capabilities

Practice Exercise 77 - Select and Mask

1. *File Menu→Open→C:\Data\PhotoshopCC-2\Allie Zack.jpg→* Open .
2. **Select Allie and Zack using the Object Select Tool:** *Object Select Tool→Select Allie→Hold the* Shift *key and Select Zack→Both Allie and Zack should be selected.*
3. **Choose** *Rectangular Marquee Tool→ Add To Selection→Select any other area that needs to be added to the selection.*
4. **Choose the Layer Mask** *(located at the bottom of the Layers Panel).*

5. *Select Menu→Select and Mask→View Mode* View Mode →
   Tip: Or click on the **Select and Mask** button located within the **Rectangular Marquee** options.
6. *Select the Zoom Tool to identify specific areas.*
7. *Select the Hand Tool to move an area.*
8. **Adjust the Shift Edge: -10%**
   Tip: Notice a negative % removes a selection edge and a positive % adds to a selection edge.
9. **Adjust the Contrast: 10%:**
10. **Test It:** *Make other adjustments as desired and view the results.*

Practice Exercise 78 - Jagged edge

1. *File Menu→Open→C:\Data\PhotoshopCC-2\Allie Zack.jpg→* Open .
2. *Magic Wand Tool→ Select the purple sweater→* Select and Mask... *button→ Zoom in to "clothing" located on the top left side of the Select and Mask interface.*

3. **Test It:** *Adjust Edge Detection: Radius.*
4. **Test It:** *Global Refinements: Smooth.*
5. **Test It:** *Global Refinements: Feather.*
6. **Test It:** *Global Refinements: Contrast.*
7. **Test It:** *Global Refinements: Shift Edge.*

Practice Exercise 79 - Fine-Tune Hair

1. *File Menu→Open→C:\Data\PhotoshopCC-2\Old Image.png→* Open .
2. *Polygon Selection Tool→Select the hair area→* Select and Mask... *Button.*

Chapter 6 - Masking Capabilities

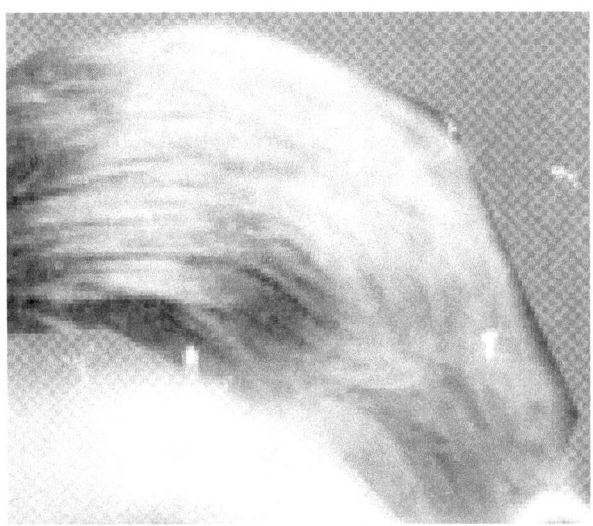

3. Use the Hand Tool to move around.
4. Use the Zoom tool to zoom in.
5. Use the Refine Edge Brush to repair the edge of the hair area.

Section 2: Quick Mask

Section Table Of Contents:
6.9 Quick Mask Painting
6.10 Quick Mask Background Color.

6.9 Quick Mask Painting

This is a fine-tuning selection technique that allows you to paint a selection around hard-to-select areas. When the **Quick Mask** mode is active, the **Brush Tool** is used to add or subtract selections by pressing the icon to switch between foreground and background.

Tip: In the following icon, **Black** is the foreground and **White** is background. When you press the icon, **White** becomes foreground and **Black** becomes the background.

The **Quick Mask** mode button is located at the bottom of the **Tools Panel**.

Practice Exercise 80 - Quick Mask Painting

1. *File Menu →Open →C:\Data\PhotoshopCC-2\Boy.jpg→* .
2. *Magnetic Lasso Tool →Lasso the boy's head only.*
3. *Quick Mask mode : Press the so the color pallet looks like and the Quick Mask Mode should look like →Brush Tool →Size: 45 →Paint the boy's neck to reveal more selection.*
4. *Click the Quick Mask mode to see election results.*
5. *Click the Quick Mask mode →Switch background to White → Brush Tool →Paint the neck to see the inverse selection.*
6. *Use Quick Mask mode to see the results.*

6.10 Quick Mask Background Color

Sometimes, the **Quick Mask Background Color** is too close to a background of an image. By changing it, the color is easier to view.

Practice Exercise 81 - Quick Mask background color change

Continue from the previous practice exercise:

Double click on the Quick Mask mode → ***Double click on the color box*** →***R:0, G: 255, B: 0*** → OK → OK → ***Quick Mask mode*** to see the green background.

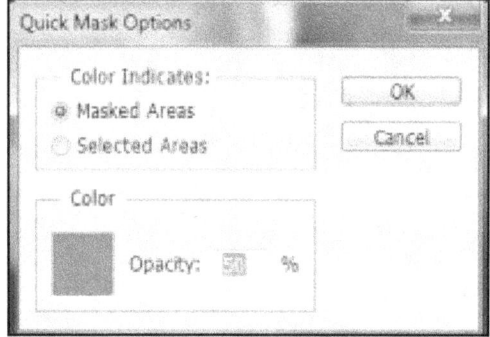

Section 3: Layer Mask

The white area in the example below represents a selected area. The dark area represents an unselected area.

Section Table Of Contents:
   6.11 Reveal Selection
   6.12 Hide Selection
   6.13 Replace Sky

6.11 Reveal Selection

The white area will be revealed in the center of a square.
Select object→Layer→Layer Mask→Reveal Selection.

Tip: the **Reveal Selection** icon can also be found on the bottom of the **Layers Panel**.

Student Project D - Layer Mask Reveal Selection

1. *File Menu→Open→C:\Data\PhotoshopCC-2\Guitar Wood.jpg→* Open .
2. *File Menu→Open→C:\Data\PhotoshopCC-2\Backdrop.jpg→* Open .
3. *Minimize the Backdrop.jpg → Move Tool →Move backdrop to Guitar Wood.jpg →Double-click on the Background layer to change the name to Layer 0→* OK .
4. **Set up the layers:**

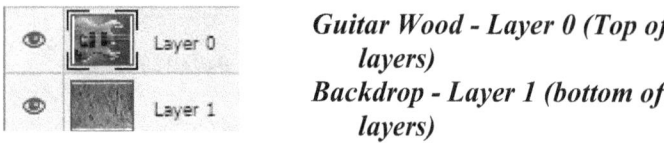

   Guitar Wood - Layer 0 (Top of layers)
   Backdrop - Layer 1 (bottom of layers)

5. *Select Guitar Wood-Layer 0→Select the Magic Wand Tool →Tolerance: 32→Select the Blue background of Layer 0 (Guitar Wood Layer).* **Tip**: You may need to click it several times.

Chapter 6 - Masking Capabilities

6. *Select →Inverse. (the guitar should be selected)*
7. *Select layer 0 →Layer →Layer Mask → Reveal Selection.*

6.12 Hide Selection

The dark area will be exposed (you will see the image in the layer below), and the unselected area layer will then be visible.

Select object →Layer Menu →Layer Mask →Hide Selection.

Student Project E - Layer Mask Hide Selection

1. *File Menu→Open→C:\Data\PhotoshopCC-2\Executive.jpg→* Open .
2. *File Menu→Open→C:\Data\PhotoshopCC-2\Landscape.jpg→* Open .
3. *Minimize the Landscape.jpg → Move Tool →Move Landscape.jpg to Executive.jpg →Double-click on the Background layer to rename it to Layer 0→ OK .*
4. **Set up the layers:**

   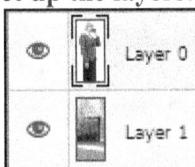

   Executive.jpg (layer 0 top)

   Landscape.jpg (Layer 1 bottom)

5. *Use the Magic Wand Tool to select the white background of the Executive.*
6. *Use the Quick Mask mode with the Brush Tool to fine-tune the selection→Exit the Quick Mask mode .*
7. *Make sure Layer 0 is highlighted→Layer Menu →Layer Mask →Hide Selection.*

6.13 Replace Sky

This tool will **Replace** a bad **Sky** with a choice of available layouts. You can also upload your own predefined **Sky** by pressing the ⊞ on the bottom of the "**Select Replacement Sky**" presets dropdown. Once added you can return to the **Select Replacement Sky Presets** to use your custom image.

Practice Exercise 82 - Replace Sky

1. *File menu →Open →C:\Data\PhotoshopCC-2\Harbor.jpg→* Open .

2. *Edit menu →Sky Replacement →Choose Sky preset →*
3. *Adjust Shift Edge to add or remove more details.*

   Shift Edge   -22

4. *Zoom in using the Zoom Tool located in the Sky Replacement dialog box and adjust the brightness slider. The tools will affect other objects in the image.*

   Brightness   0

Page 83

5. **Get more Sky Presets:** *Edit menu →Sky Replacement →Choose Sky preset →*

   → Gear →Get More Skies →Download Free Skys →In a Web Browser: Select a Sky preset →  *→ Save .*
6. **Return to Photoshop:** *Edit menu →Sky Replacement →Choose Sky preset →*

   Gear →Get More Skies →Download Free Skies →Select the download preset.
7. **To Load new downloaded presets:** *Gear →Get More Skies →Import Presets.*

Tip: Follow the procedures above and apply **Replace Sky** to the following images: **Countryside.jpg** and **Landscape.jpg**.

Tip: Another command to consider is *Select Menu →Sky.*

Section 4: Clipping Mask

A **Clipping Mask** is a group of layers that eliminate parts of an image and display other areas defined by a mask area. The images on a lower layer are visible, but only specific parts of the upper layer will show through to be visible.

Section Table Of Contents
   6.14 Clipping Mask

6.14 Clipping Mask

This allows you to view the top layer through an object on the background layer.

Student Project F - Clipping Mask

1. *File Menu →Open →C:\Data\PhotoshopCC-2\Two Flowers.jpg→ Open .*
2. *Rename the background layer to Layer 0. (Double click on Background).*
3. *Create Type Layer: Horizontal Type Tool T →Draw a text box on top of the flowers →Type the word: FLOWER →Change the Font Size: 140.*
4. *Arrange and rename the layers as follows:*
5. *Create a Clipping Mask:*
   Select Layer: Layer 0 → Layer Menu → Create Clipping Mask.
6. *Move flower layer: Select Layer0 →Move Tool →Move Flower layer.*

Student Project G - Clipping Mask

1. *File Menu →Open →C:\Data\PhotoshopCC-2\Landscape.jpg→ Open .*
2. *File Menu →Open →C:\Data\PhotoshopCC-2\Logo.png→ Open .*

3. *File Menu→Open→C:\Data\PhotoshopCC-2\Backdrop.jpg→* Open .
4. **Combine Files:** *Move Logo.jpg and Backdrop.jpg to Landscape.jpg. (use the Move Tool*)
5. *Rename and rearrange the layers as follows:*

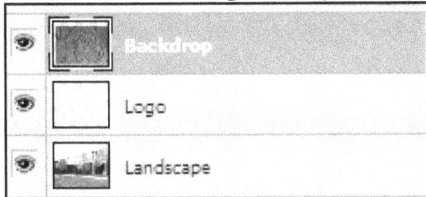

6. **Create Clipping mask:** *Select Backdrop layer→Layer Menu→Create Clipping Mask*
7. *Select the Logo layer and use the Move Tool →Move the Logo to the top of the building.*

Student Project H - Clipping Mask

1. *File Menu→Open→C:\Data\PhotoshopCC-2\Boy.jpg→* Open .
2. *File Menu→Open→C:\Data\PhotoshopCC-2\Countryside.jpg→* Open .
3. **Combine files:** *Move Conntryside.jpg to Boy.jpg.*
4. *Rename the background layer to Layer 0. (Double click on Background).*
5. **Select Layers:** *Select both sunglass lenses on the Boy layer.*
   Tip: You may need to temporarily deselect the eye on the **Landscape** layer in order to view the **Boy** Layer.
   Select Layer 0→Layer Menu→New→Layer via Copy.
6. **Adjust Layers:** *Select the Countryside layer→ Layer Menu→ Create Clipping Mask.*

Chapter 6 - Masking Capabilities

7. *Select the Countryside layer→Image Menu→ Adjustments →Brightness/Contrast→Darken the layer→* OK .
8. **Move Layer:** *Move Tool→Select Layer1 →Move countryside to find the best position.*

Section 5: Advanced Techniques

This is an **Artificial Intelligence (AI) Tool** that, when selection is moved to a new location, will patch the original location with the surrounding background image. There are several options: **Content-Aware Scale**, **Move** and **Fill**.

Section Table Of Contents:
    6.15 Content-Aware Scale
    6.16 Content-Aware Move Tool
    6.17 Content-Aware Fill
    6.18 Puppet Warp Tool.

6.15 Content-Aware Scale

This command scales an image while maintaining the ratio of a selected object (such as a boat, building, or people). The *Edit→Transform→Scale* will affect all pixels and information. The **Content-Aware Scale** will attempt to keep the selected object intact. *Edit→Content-Aware*.

Practice Exercise 83 - Content-Aware Scale

1. *File Menu →Open →C:\Data\PhotoshopCC-2\ContentAwareScale.jpg→* Open .
2. *Select the Boat→Select→Save Selection→Name: Boat→Select→Deselect or* Ctrl D .
3. *Select the entire document: Select the menu→All.*
4. *Edit→Content-Aware Scale →Scale the document from both sides.*

6.16 Content-Aware Move Tool

 This will quickly **Move** an image and fill the hole with existing background scenery.

Practice Exercise 84 - Content-Aware Move Tool

1. *File Menu →Open →C:\Data\PhotoshopCC-2\Running.jpg→* Open .
2. *Select the lady using the Quick Selection Tool.*
3. *Choose the "Select and Mask" button in the Selection Tool options to fine tune the selection.*
4. *Content-Aware Move Tool (Located under the Healing Tools) →Move the selected image (Press the ✓ in the Options Bar.*
5. *Use the Clone Stamp Tool to clean up the old area.*
6. **Test It:** *Open file ContentAwareScale.jpg and move one of the boats.*
7. **Test It:** *Open file Cup 3D.jpg and move the cup.*

6.17 Content-Aware Fill

This will quickly replace an image or create a new one.

Practice Exercise 85 - Content-Aware Fill

File Menu →Open →C:\Data\PhotoshopCC-2\Harbor.jpg→ Open .
Select the sky using the Quick Selection Tool →Edit→Fill→Content-Aware→Color Burn

6.18 Puppet Warp Tool

This is a technique used to warp or move the edge of an object.
Edit Menu→Puppet Warp. Version CS5+ Feature.

Practice Exercise 86 - Puppet Warp

1. *File Menu→Open→C:\Data\PhotoshopCC-2\Beach.jpg→* Open .
2. *Zoom to the shoreline→Select the sand along the shoreline as well as the bushes using the Polygon Selection Tool→*

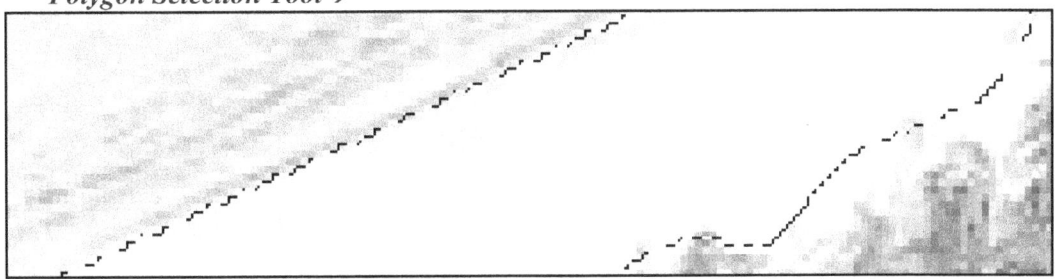

3. *Layer Menu→New→Layer via Copy.*
4. *Edit Menu→Puppet Warp→Place pins between the sand and shoreline defining the mesh→ Move the pinpoints around to redefine the shoreline.*

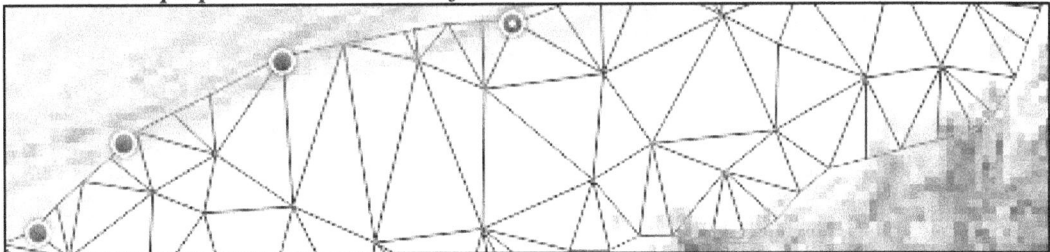

Use the Alt *key to remove points. Mac CS6: Use the* option *key.* **(If that doesn't work, try the** command **and** shift **keys).**

5. **Options Bar →** ✓ *commit puppet warp.*
6. **Test It:** Try the **Puppet Warp Tool** on **Sea Cliff.jpg** or **Bridge Colored.jpg**.

Chapter 7 - Text Layer Effects

This chapter will cover techniques used to manipulate text including warping and shaping. **Adobe** uses the word **Type** when referring to text which means **Typography**.

Chapter Contents:
Section 1: Text Formatting - **Character** and **Paragraph Panels** format **Text Layers**.
Section 2: Reshape Text Path - This will allow text to appear on angles and curved shapes.
Section 3: Layer Comps - This will allow multiple layouts to be defined.
Section 4: Vanishing Point - This will adjust text on a 3D angle.

Section 1: Text Formatting

This will review the capabilities in the **Options Toolbar**, **Character**, and **Paragraph Panel**.

Practice Exercise 87 - Text Formatting

File Menu→New→Print→Choose 8-1/2 X 11 page.
Horizontal Type tool→draw a text box and enter some text.

7.1 Type Options

Many options on the **Type** options bar are also located in the **Character Panel** below.

7.2 Character Panel

This panel can be displayed by: *Window Menu→Character*.

    A - **Font Family** - This is also called **Typeface** and some examples are: **Arial, Times New Roman**, etc. Each **Font Family** may have a different set of variations such as **Regular, Bold, Italic,** or **Bold/Italic,** etc. These variations of the **Font Family** can be changed in the many above **Options Bar** under the **Bold** dropdown arrow. **Arial** has 9 different variations comparted to **Times New Roman** which has 4 and **Marlett** has only one (Regular).

    B - **Font Size** - This is the **Size** of the text. The value can be typed in or chosen from the pull-down menu.

    C - **Kerning** - This will adjust a specified **distance between characters** that overlap. For example, WA can be kerned so the W and A fit closer together. This feature is used to better fit a title on a line by bringing all characters closer together. To turn it off: choose 0. **Tip**: Some common kerning examples are: **LA, P., To, Tr, Ta, Tu, Te, Ty, Wa, WA, We, Wo, Ya, and Yo.**

    D - **Vertical Scale** - This **Scales Text (Type) Characters** larger or smaller in a **Vertical** direction.

    E - **Baseline** - This will allow you to move a selected character up or down within a specific distance from the **Baseline**. (2nd shifts upward and Log_{23} shifts downward).

    F - **Font Style** - These are **Character Types** such as **Regular, Italic, Bold, Bold Italic.**

    G - **Leading** - This will increase or decrease the space between two lines *W1→Enter Key→W2→Select both→Change the Leading value.*

Chapter 7 - Text Layer Effects

H - **Tracking** - This will adjust the space between letters. In other words, it loosens or tightens a block of text, not affecting **Kerning.**

I - **Horizontal** - This will scale the **Character's** larger or smaller text in a horizontal direction.

J - **Color** - This will change the **Color** of the text.

K - **Type Options** - These will include **Faux Bold, Faux Italic, All Caps, Small Caps, Superscript, Subscript, Underline,** and **Strikethrough.**

L - **Font Options** - These are the different **Characters** available:

M - **Anti-aliasing** - This feature includes: **None, Sharp, Crisp, Strong, Smooth, Windows LCD,** and **Windows.**

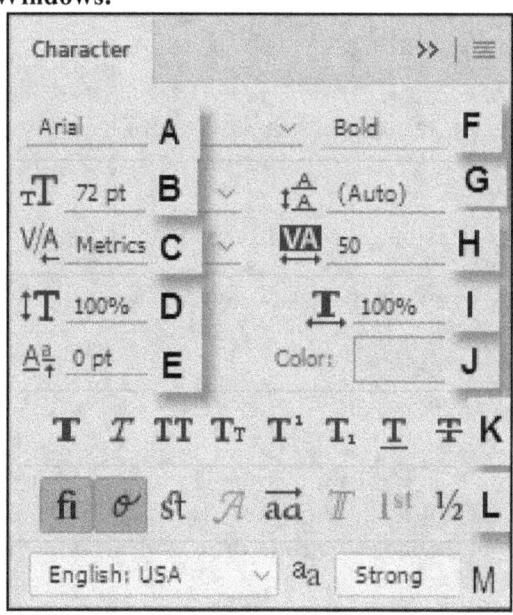

7.3 Paragraph Panel

This **Panel** can be displayed by: *Window Menu→Paragraph.*

A - **Align Text** - This will align **Text (Type) Characters** such as **Left to Right, Center,** and **Right to Left.**

B - **Justification** - This will stretch text at the end of a margin. The options available include **Justify Last Left, Justify Last Center, Justify Last Right,** and **Justify All.**

C - **Indent** - This indents a **Paragraph** by a specific amount of space on the left which affects the entire paragraph. The **Indent** options available are **Indent Left Margin, Indent Right Margin,** and **Indent First Line.**

D - **Paragraph Spacing** - This will adjust a **Paragraph** above and below text in **Paragraph.** The options available include **Add Space Before Paragraph,** and **Add Space After Paragraph.**

E - **Hyphenate CheckBox** - This turns on the ability to continue a word on the next line. Example: think-ing.

Chapter 7 - Text Layer Effects

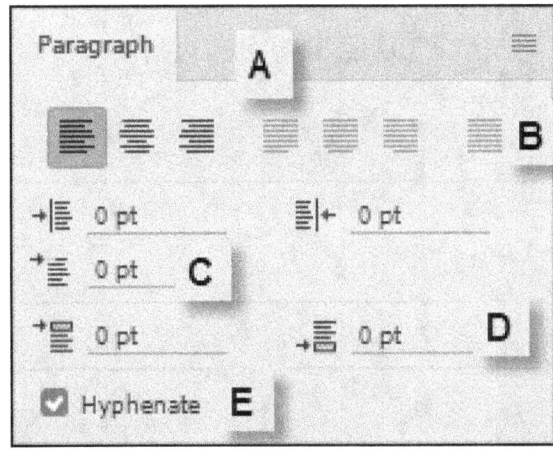

7.4 Transform Text Box

This will adjust or move anchor points of the text.
Horizontal Type Tool→Draw a text box→Enter the text→Edit→Free Transform→
(Move anchor points using your mouse to scale or destort the letters)

Section 2: Reshape Text Path

7.5 Pen Tool

The **Pen Tool** can be used to create unique curves that would be almost impossible to create using a **Free Form Tool** such as a **Pencil**.

Practice Exercise 88 - Pen

File Menu→Open→C:\Data\PhotoshopCC-2\BabyBracelet.Jpg→ Open .
Pen Tool→Click inside near the left heart→Click inside near the right heart and drag the mouse down to create a curve inside the bracelet→ Click the Horizontal Type Tool T *→Click on the front part of the curve (When you get near the path, the cursor will change)→Type: Baby Bracelet.*

7.6 Freeform Tool

This draws a pin line in a controlled freehand direction.

Practice Exercise 89 - Freeform

File Menu→Open→C:\Data\PhotoshopCC-2\Alaska Island.jpg→ Open .
Freeform Pen Tool→Draw free form in the sky around the mountains→ Click the Horizontal Type Tool T *→Click in the middle of the line→Type: Alaska Misty Fjord Island.*

7.7 Add Anchor Point Tool

This adds **Anchor Points** to **Pen** and **Freeform** curves in order to modify the curvature and make necessary adjustments.

Practice Exercise 90 - Anchor Point

1. *File Menu→New→Print Tab→Print Presets→Letter (8.5 x 11 in @ 300 ppi→* Create.
   →Pen Tool→Point 1→Point 2 (drag down to draw curve)→Point 3(drag down to draw a curve).

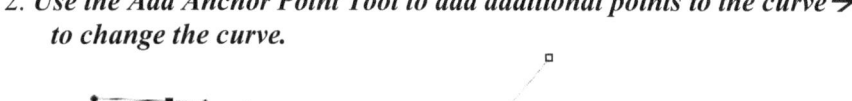

2. *Use the Add Anchor Point Tool to add additional points to the curve→ Move those anchor points to change the curve.*

7.8 Delete Anchor Point Tool

This deletes the **Anchor Points** to the **Pen** and **Freeform** curves in order to modify the curvature and make adjustments as necessary.

7.9 Convert Point Tool

This is used to change the direction of the next **Pen Anchor Point**.

Practice Exercise 91 - Convert Point

File Menu →New→Print Tab→Print Presets→Letter (8.5 x 11 in @ 300 ppi→ Create.
Pen Tool→Draw a square box using 4 points using the Pen Tool→Switch to the Convert Point Tool→Click on the corners when the cursor changes to the Corner Point Tool→Round the corners.

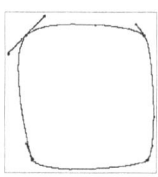

7.10 Path Selection Tool

This moves the entire **Pen Path**.

7.11 Direct Selection Tool

This moves **Anchor Points** within the path.

Practice Exercise 92 - Path and Direct Selection

    File Menu → New → Print Tab → Print Presets → Letter (8.5 x 11 in @ 300 ppi → Create.
    Pen Tool → Draw a path → Choose the Add Anchor Point Tool → Add an Anchor Point in the middle of the path (Add Anchor Point Tool) → Use the Path Selection Tool to move the path → Use the Direct Selection Tool to move the ends of an Anchor Point.

7.12 Warp Text Options Bar

This will **Warp** selected **Text** using different shapes.

    File Menu → New → Print Tab → Print Presets → Letter (8.5 x 11 in @ 300 ppi → Create.
    Warp Text: *Horizontal Type Tool → Draw a box and type in some text: This Is Text → Option Bar → Create warped text button → Warp text dialog box drop-down → Choose desired warp Arc → OK → Commit. Also, you can use the Type Menu → Warp Text.*

Practice Exercise 93 - Warp Text

1. *File Menu → Open → C:\Data\PhotoshopCC-2\Sunlight Detergent.psd → Open.*
2. *Horizontal Type Tool → Select the text Sunlight! on the work area → Select the Sunlight! Layer.*
3. *In the Options Bar, locate the Create warped text button → Warp text dialog box drop-down → Choose desired warp.* 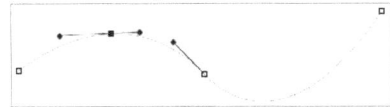 *→ OK → Commit.*

Tip: Perform the same options to the "Super Clean Formula" layer.

7.13 Warp Text

This will display various **Warp** styles.

Practice Exercise 94 - Wrap text on a path

    File Menu → New → Print Tab → Print Presets → Letter (8.5 x 11 in @ 300 ppi → Create.
    Horizontal Type Tool → Type the text "This is a test."
    Type Menu → Warp Text → Arc → Adjust controls.

Practice Exercise 95 - Warp text on a path

    File Menu → Open → C:\Data\PhotoshopCC-2\Sunlight Detergent.psd → Open.
    Review text "130 FL.OZ." text and Skew text to the right → Select Layer → Edit Menu → Transform → Skew → Drag upper right transfer handle → Commit.

Chapter 7 - Text Layer Effects

Section 3: Layer Comps

7.14 Layer Comps

This allows you to create different design layouts and compares them to determine the best possibilities. *New→Layer Comp*.

Student Project I - Layer Comps

1. *File Menu→Open→C:\Data\PhotoshopCC-2\Sunlight Detergent.psd→* `Open` .
2. *Window Menu→ Layer Comp*.
3. *Create a new Layer Comp ▭ →Layer Comp1: Check all 3 options→* `OK` .
   Move Tool→Select Sunlight! layer→Move text up.
   Move Tool→Select Super Clean Formula layer→Move text down.
4. *Create a new Layer Comp ▭ →Layer Comp 2: Check all 3 options→* `OK` .
   Move Tool→Select Fresh Mint Scent layer→Move text to the left.
   Move Tool→Select 130 FL. OZ. layer→Move text to the right.
   Layer Comp 2

5. *Create a new Layer Comp ▭ →Layer comp 3: Check all 3 options→* `OK` .
   Select Super Clean Formula layer→Type Menu→Warp Text→ Style: Arch.
   Layer Comp 3

6. *Create new Layer Comp→Layer comp 4: Check all 3 options→* `OK` .
   Layer Comp 4

7. *Use the arrow button on the bottom of the Layer Comp Panel* ◄▬▬► *to switch between Layer Comps.*

Section 4: Vanishing Point

7.15 Vanishing Point

This allows you to place text in a 3D perspective image.
Filter Menu→Vanishing Point.

Student Project J - Vanishing Point1

1. ***File Menu→Open→C:\Data\PhotoshopCC-2\Art_Cube.png→*** Open .
2. ***File Menu→Open→C:\Data\PhotoshopCC-2\Art_Cube_text.png→*** Open .
3. **Art_Cube_Text:** *Select Menu →All→ Edit Menu →Copy.*
4. **Art_Cube.png:** *Filter Menu →Vanishing Point →Draw Vanishing Point Area (Top of the box)→Make sure you are in the Vanishing Point Editor →* Ctrl V *→Position Text on the box.* **Mac CS6:** *Use the* Command V *keys.*

Student Project K - Vanishing Point2

Create a label for the cup to read "Coffee Cup" or "Hot Cocoa Cup" using the **Pen Tool**, **Warp Text**, **Warp Text on a Path**, and **Vanishing Point**.

File Menu→Open→C:\Data\PhotoshopCC-2\Cup 3D.jpg→ Open .
Layer Panel Menu ▤ *→ Duplicate (* Ctrl J *) →*
Layer Panel Menu ▤ *→Duplicate(* Ctrl J *) →*
Layer Panel Menu ▤ *→Duplicate(* Ctrl J *) →*
Layer Panel Menu ▤ *→Duplicate(* Ctrl J *) →*
Use a different effect on each layer.

Chapter 8 - Advanced Features

Adobe has added some unique advanced **Artificial Intelligence** (**AI**) features to its suite including **Video** and **3D Tools**.

Chapter Contents:
Section 1: Neural Filters - These are new Artificial Intelligence (AI) tools.
Section 2: Actions - This will allow you to record several operations into one command.
Section 3: Video Editing - This will allow you to edit a video clip.
Section 4: 3D Objects - This will allow you to edit 3D objects.

Section 1: Neural Filters

This new **Artificial Intelligence (AI)** driven **Tool** will adjust images based on program rules. You will see the "Processing…" message appears, which, in some cases, takes a few minutes to install. If a filter is not installed, click the gray cloud until the following appears: . Also, a couple of very useful tools include **Colorize** and **Smart Portrait**. *Filter Menu→* Neural Filters... . *If a screen seems frozen, it might be processing. However, you can click in the Options Bar to review the status.*

8.1 Skin Smoothing

Skin Smoothing This filter is designed to **Smooth** facial blemishes, skin spots, and acne without blurring other areas of a face. **Tip**: The eyes and hair will not be affected by this filter.

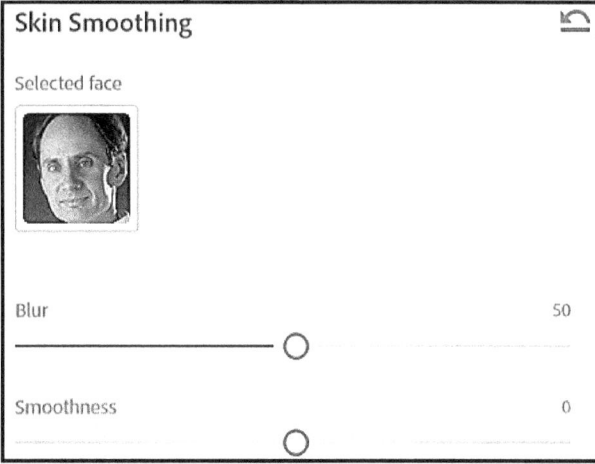

Practice Exercise 96 - Skin Smoothing

1. *File Menu→Open→C:\Data\PhotoshopCC-2\Face Wrinkles.jpg→* Open .
2. *Filter Menu→Neural Filters→Turn on Skin Smoothing→Blur: 64→Smoothness: +46→*

3. *Turn on/off the Eye icon in Layer 1 to compare the difference:*

Chapter 8 - Advanced Features

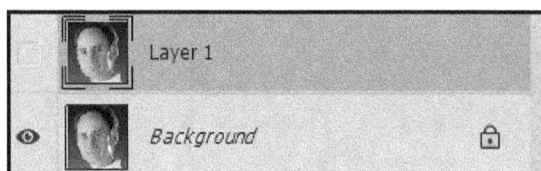

4. **Test It:** *Turn on/off the* 👁 *Eye icon in the Layers Panel to compare the differences:*

8.2 Smart Portrait

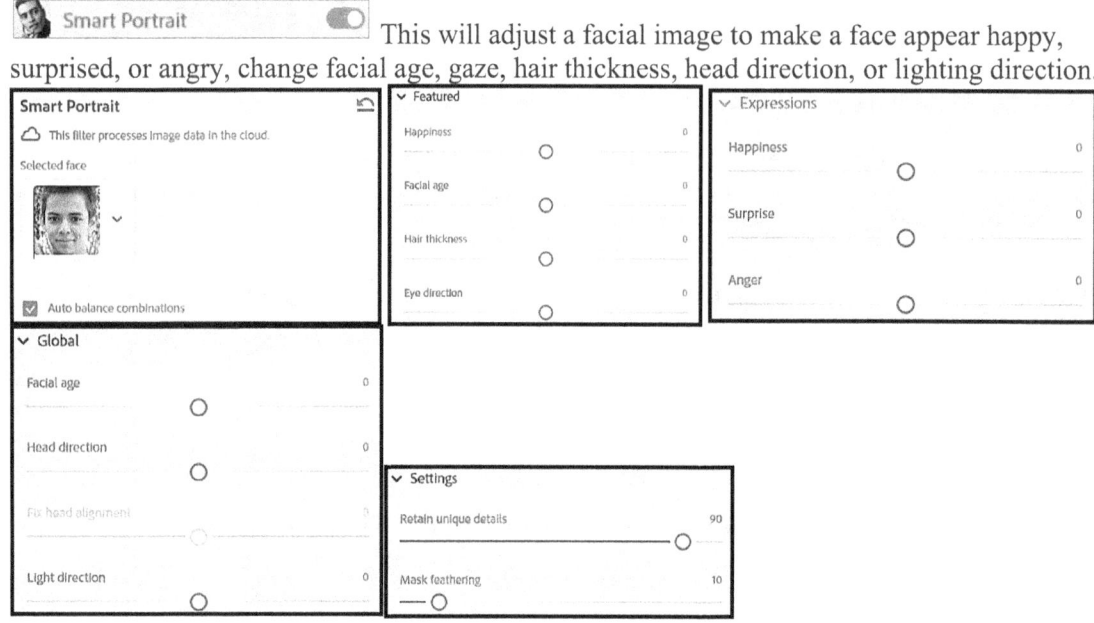

This will adjust a facial image to make a face appear happy, surprised, or angry, change facial age, gaze, hair thickness, head direction, or lighting direction.

Practice Exercise 97 - Smart Portrait

1. *File Menu→Open→C:\Data\PhotoshopCC-2\Allie Zack.jpg→* Open .
2. *Filter Menu→Neural Filters→Turn on* 🔘 *Smart Portrait.*

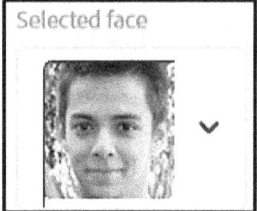

3. *Select desired Face:*
4. **Happiness Slider:** *A positive number makes a face appear happy, and a negative number makes a face appear sad:*

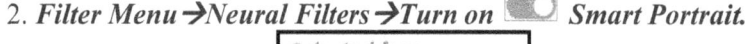

5. **Facial Age Slider.** *A positive number makes a face appear older and a Negative number makes a face appear younger:*

6. **Hair Thickness Slider.** *A positive number makes hair thicker, and a negative number makes hair thinner:*

7. **Eye Direction Slider.** *A positive number makes a face look to the right and a negative number makes a face look to the left.*

    Eye direction   0

8. **Surprise Slider.** *A positive number makes a face appear Surprised and a negative number makes a face appear shocked.*

    Surprise   0

9. **Anger Slider.** *A positive number makes a face appear Angry and a negative number makes a face appear happy.*

    Anger   0

10. **Head Direction Slider.** *A positive number makes a head look to the right and a negative number makes a head look to the left.*

    Head direction   0

11. *Choose Output Options:* ☑ Output as new color layer → Output: New layer → **OK**.

8.3 Makeup Transfer

Makeup Transfer This will apply **Makeup** to the eyes and mouth area from one image to another.

Practice Exercise 98 - Makeup Transfer

1. *File Menu →Open →C:\Data\PhotoshopCC-2\Maestro.jpg→* Open .
2. *File Menu →Open →C:\Data\PhotoshopCC-2\Executive.jpg→* Open .
3. *Open Executive →Filter Menu →Neural Filters →Turn on* **Makeup Transfer**.
4. *Select the Image Maestro.jpg*

5. **Close Makeup Transfer:** Output: New layer → **OK**.
6. *The end result may be different than you expect:*

    Before Filter: **After Filter:**

8.4 Landscape Mixer

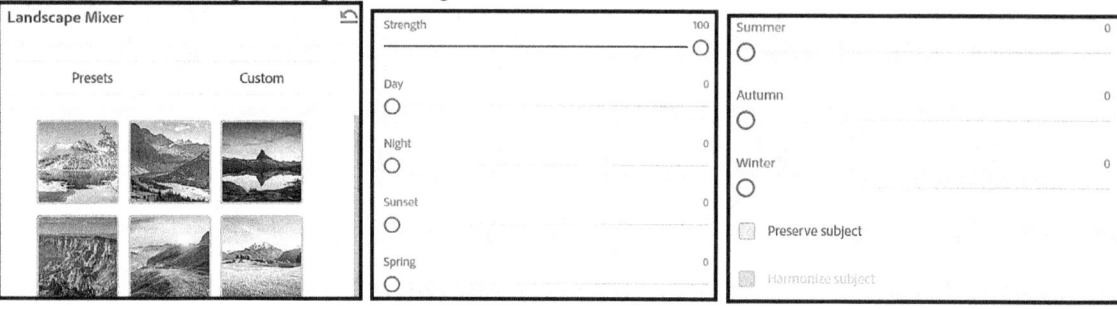 This will allow you to adjust all backgrounds of **Landscape** images. It will combine an image with preset images available.

Practice Exercise 99 - Landscape Mixer

1. *File Menu→Open→C:\Data\PhotoshopCC-2\Countryside.jpg→* Open .
2. *Filter Menu→Neural Filters→Turn on* 🔘 *Landscape Mixer.*

3. **Select the snow scene:**
4. **The higher the strength, the more snow will appear:**

5. **Adjust the following to see the effect: Night, Day, Sunset, Spring, Summer, Autumn, and Winter.**
6. **Close Landscape Mixer:** Output New layer → **OK** .
7. **The following will be the result:**

8.5 Style Transfer

Style Transfer 🔘 This will apply an image **Style** to a photo in order to change the contour or entire image for the creation of a new look and layout.

Chapter 8 - Advanced Features

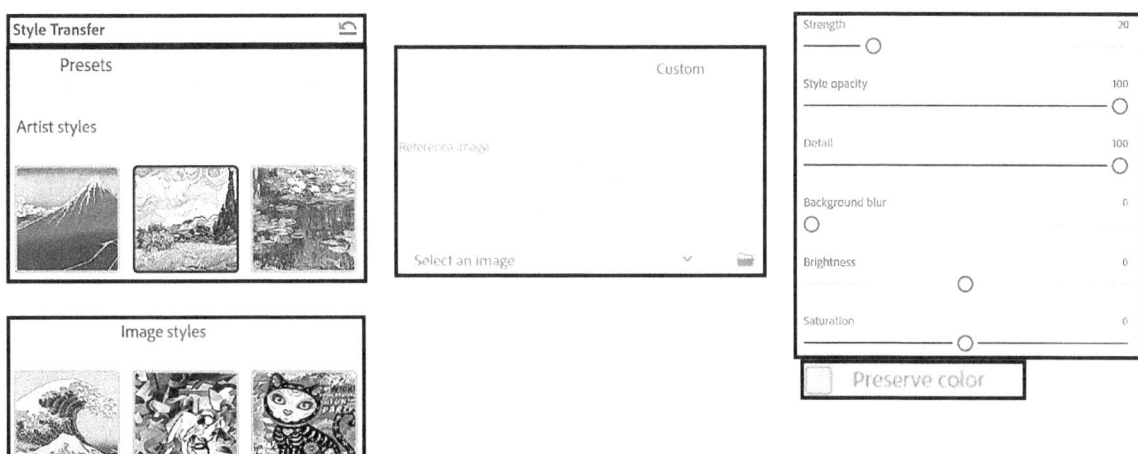

Practice Exercise 100 - Style Transfer

1. *File Menu→Open→C:\Data\PhotoshopCC-2\Beach.jpg→* `Open`.
2. *Filter Menu→Neural Filters→Turn on* Style Transfer.

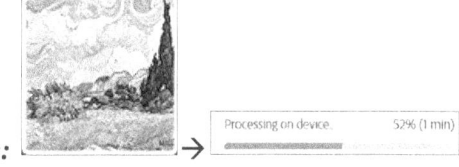

3. *Choose the following Style to transfer to an image:*
4. *Adjust the following to view effect: Strength, Style Opacity, Detail, Background Blur, Brightness, Saturation, and Preserve Color.*
5. **Close Style Transfer:** `Output New layer` → `OK`.
6. *Layer 1 is the result of the Style Transfer:*

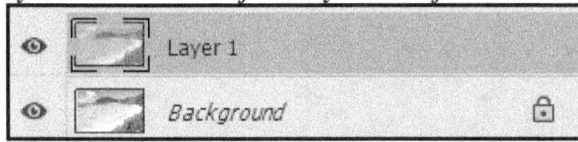

7. *The final results will look similar to the following:*

8.6 Harmonize

Harmonization When you place an object on a different layer, the shading of the image may not match the background. This feature will shade the new object to match the background. However, layers will *not* be merged if you choose **New Layer**. You must isolate the

Chapter 8 - Advanced Features

object on a **Layer Mask** before beginning the program. Select an object on the layer and choose **Mask** (located at the bottom of the **Layers Panel**). *Filter menu→Neural Filter→Harmonization.*

 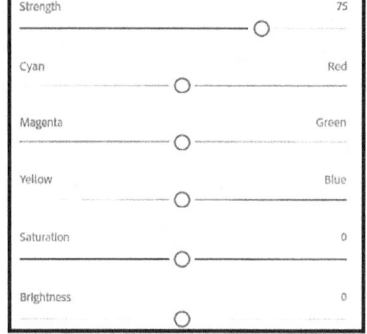

Practice Exercise 101 - Harmonize

1. *File Menu→Open →C:\Data\PhotoshopCC-2\Allie Zack.jpg→* Open .
2. *Select Allie and Zack using the Object Select Tool:* Object Select Tool→Select Allie→Hold the Shift key and Select Zack→Both Allie and Zack should be selected.
3. *Choose Rectangular Marquee Tool→ Add To Selection→Select any other area that needs to be added to the selection.*
4. *Choose the Layer Mask (located at the bottom of the Layers Panel).*

5. *File Menu→Open→C:\Data\PhotoshopCC-2\Countryside.jpg→* Open .
6. *Use the Move Tool to move Allie Zack.jpg into the Countryside.jpg.*

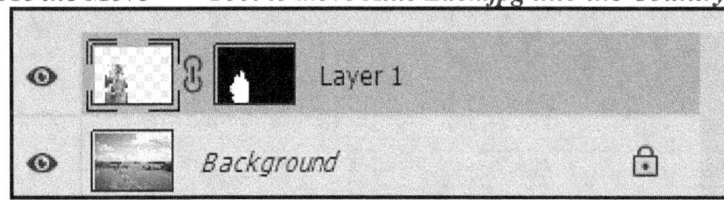

7. *Make Allie and Zack larger: Edit menu→Free Transform→Adjust the size and move them down to the bottom edge of the Countryside.*

8. *Filter Menu→Neural Filters→Turn on Harmonize.*
9. *Select a layer* [Select a layer] *→Select Countryside.jpg→*
10. *Adjust the Strength to match the color shading:*

Chapter 8 - Advanced Features

11. *Adjust the following as desired to see the effect: Cyan/Red, Magenta/Green, Yellow/Blue, Saturation, and Brightness.*
12. **Close Harmonize:** Output New layer → **OK**.
13. *Layer results will look similar to the following:*

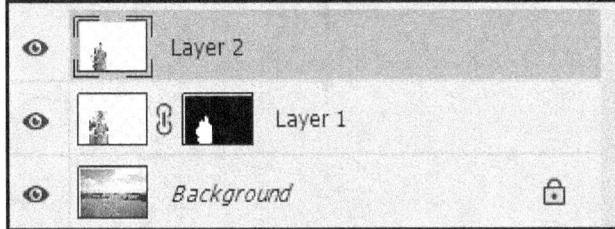

8.7 Color Transfer

This will allow you to **Transfer** a reference image to a particular image as well as apply color shading. You can adjust the brightness, saturation, and luminescence and also choose from standard preset images to customize results.

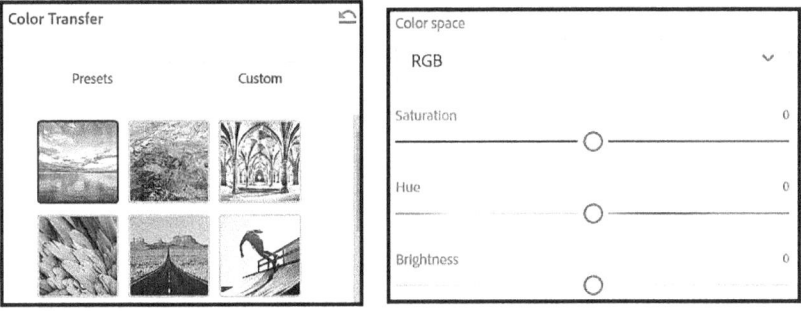

Practice Exercise 102 - Color Transfer

1. *File Menu→Open→C:\Data\PhotoshopCC-2\Countryside.jpg→* Open.
2. *Filter Menu→Neural Filters→Turn on* ⬤ *Color Transfer.*
3. *Select the following image to transfer:*
4. **Close Color Transfer:** Output New layer → **OK**.
5. *The layers will look similar to the following:*

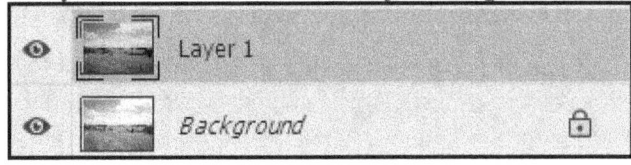

8.8 Colorize

Colorize ⬤ This will add color to black and white images. First, identify one or many focal points of interest (such as the face) and enhance that area with color attributes. Because faded over or underexposed images may result in less accurate color enhancements, use one of the **Healing Tools** to repair any flaws.

 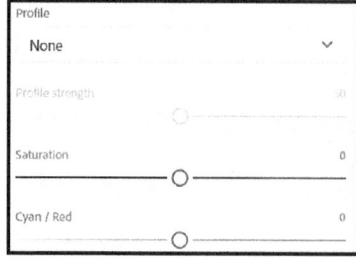 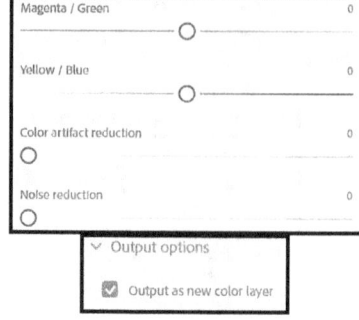

Practice Exercise 103 - Colorize

1. **File Menu→Open→C:\Data\PhotoshopCC-2\Old Image.png→** `Open`.
2. **Repair any bad spots using the Spot Healing Brush Tool: Select** ▨ **Spot Healing Brush Tool→Click the white blotches on the image.**
3. **Filter Menu→Neural Filters→Turn on** ◉ **Colorize.**
4. **Select** ☑ `Auto color image`.
5. **Choose Profile: Retro Dark:** 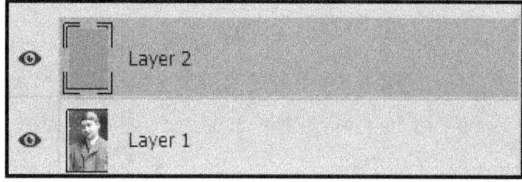.
6. **Adjust the following to see the effect: Profile, Profile Strength, Saturation, Cyan/Red, Magenta/Green, Yellow/Blue, Color Artifact Reduction, and Noise Reduction.**
7. **Choose Output Options:** ☑ `Output as new color layer` → `Output New layer` → **OK**.
8. **Turn on/off the** 👁 **Eye icon on Layer2 to compare differences:**

8.9 Super Zoom

🔍 `Super Zoom` ◉ This will allow you to **Zoom** into a specific image on a large picture and crop the **Zoomed-In** area. Any loss of resolution or quality will be automatically compensated and corrected. Use the ⊕ icon (located on the left side of the interface) to ⊕ **Zoom In** and the ⊖ to **Zoom Out**. This **AI** capability always attempts to enhance low-resolution images. However, beginning with a high-resolution image always works best. **Tip:** If you have a low-resolution picture, be sure to crop it in the original file and compare results to see which picture looks best. The **Super Zoom** will usually look better.

Chapter 8 - Advanced Features

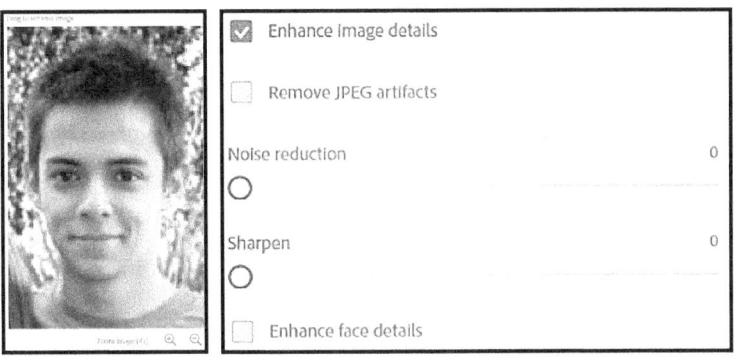

Practice Exercise 104 - Super Zoom

1. **File Menu→Open→C:\Data\PhotoshopCC-2\Allie Zack.jpg→** Open .
2. **Filter Menu→Neural Filters→Turn on** Super Zoom.
3. **Press the** Zoom and Hand Tool **to scroll around to view Zack's face. This is located in the Super Zoom interface.**
4. **Select** Enhance image details , Remove JPEG artifacts , *Sharpen to 14 points.*

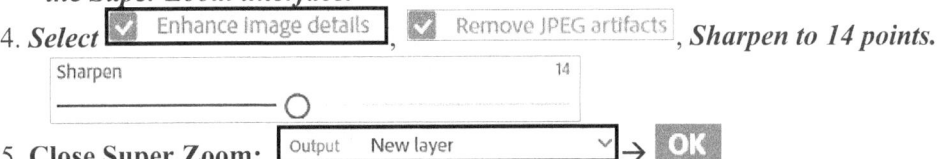

5. **Close Super Zoom:** Output New layer → **OK**
6. **Test It:** *Turn on/off the* Eye icon in the Layers Panel to compare the differences:

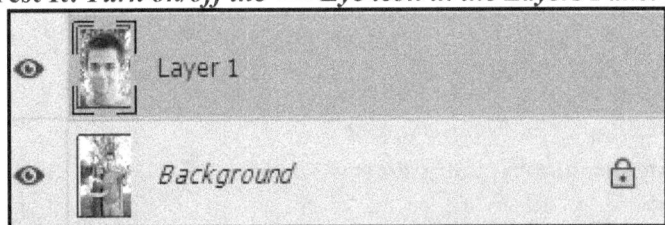

8.10 Depth Blur

Depth Blur This creates **Depth** to an image either in the foreground or background. Also, a halo or haze can be added around specific objects to make the temperature appears warmer or cooler.

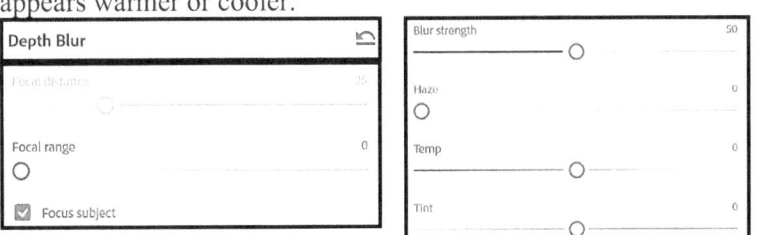

Practice Exercise 105 - Depth Blur

1. **File Menu→Open→C:\Data\PhotoshopCC-2\Twins.jpg→** Open .
2. **Filter Menu→Neural Filters→Turn on** Depth Blur.
3. **Adjust the Blur Strength:**

Page 105

Chapter 8 - Advanced Features

4. **Adjust the following to see the effect:** *Focal Range, Blur Strength, Haze, Temp, Tint, Saturation, Brightness, and Grain.*
5. **Close Depth Blur:** `Output  New layer` → **OK**.
6. **Turn on/off the** 👁 **Eye icon to compare differences between layers:**

   | 👁 | Layer 1 |
   | 👁 | Background 🔒 |

7. *The final result will be a blurred background.*

8.11 JPEG Artifacts Removal

JPEG Artifacts Removal ⚪ **Jpeg** (or .jpg) feature uses a compression technique when saving pixels to a file. When you zoom into an image, glitches (**Adobe** calls them artifacts) may be noticeable. However, this tool attempts to repair these glitches by using the strength parameter. The options available are low, medium, and high.

JPEG Artifacts Removal
Strength: High

Tip: Be sure to compare results with the original because quality could be reduced depending on the resolution and colors used.

Practice Exercise 106 - JPEG Artifacts Removal

1. *File Menu →Open →C:\Data\PhotoshopCC-2\Maestro.jpg→* `Open`.
2. *Select the Background layer→Filter Menu →Neural Filters →Turn on* ⚪ *JPEG Artifacts Removal.*
3. *Choose Strength: High:* `High` → `Processing on device... 52% (1 min)` → `Output  New layer` → **OK** → *Rename Layer to High (see below).*
4. *Select the Background layer→Filter Menu →Neural Filters →Turn on* ⚪ *JPEG Artifacts Removal.*
5. *Choose Strength: Medium:* `Medium` → `Processing on device... 52% (1 min)` → `Output  New layer` → **OK** → *Rename Layer to Medium (see below).*
6. *Select the Background layer→Filter Menu →Neural Filters →Turn on* ⚪ *JPEG Artifacts Removal.*
7. *Choose Strength: Low:* `Low` → `Processing on device... 52% (1 min)` → `Output  New layer` → **OK** →*Rename Layer to Low (see below).*
8. *Turn on/off the* 👁 *Eye icon on the High, Medium, and Low layers to compare the differences between layers:*

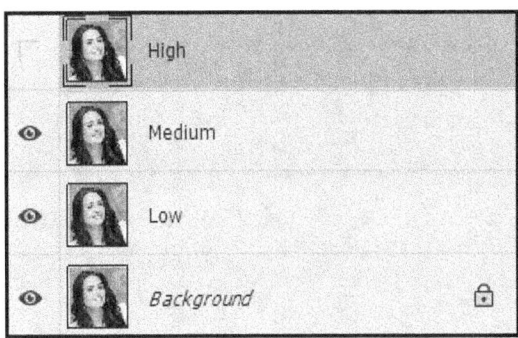

Section 2: Actions

When you press the **Play** button, an **Action** records a series of command sequences in order to create a new command. This is similar to **Microsoft Excel Macros**. It can also be used to reduce the number of steps to accomplish tasks in a shorter period of time. You will need to open the **Actions Panel** which will be covered in this section: *Window Menu →Actions.*

8.12 Actions

Adobe provides specific ways to automate steps or streamline them in a Macro style script.

Practice Exercise 107 - Run Predefined Actions

    Run the following Action: *Window Menu →Actions.*
1. *File Menu→ New →Recent Tab →Presets → Custom (7x5 in, 300 ppi, Color Mode RGB) →* `Create`.
2. **Select area**: *Rectangular Marquee Tool →Actions Panel →Molten Lead →Play Selection* ▶.
3. *File Menu →Open →C:\Data\PhotoshopCC-2\Ancestors.jpg→* `Open`.
    Action Panel →Quadrant Colors → Play Selection ▶.
4. *File Menu →Open →C:\Data\PhotoshopCC-2\Beach.jpg→* `Open`.
    Tight selection around boat: Rectangular Marquee Tool →Select Beach Layer →Action Panel →Water Reflections → Play Selection ▶.
5. *File Menu →Open →C:\Data\PhotoshopCC-2\Daniel Carina.jpg →Action Panel →Wood Frame → Play Selection* ▶.
6. *File Menu →Open →C:\Data\PhotoshopCC-2\Old Image.png→* `Open`.
    Actions Panel →Sepia Toning →Play Selection ▶.

Practice Exercise 108 - Create Action1

1. **Create Feather Blur Action**: *File Menu →Open →C:\Data\PhotoshopCC-2\Boy.jpg→* `Open`.
2. **Select the Boy's Head**: *Elliptical Marquee Tool* ⬭.
3. *Actions Pane: Create New Action* ⊞ *→Name: Blur Action →* `Record`.
4. *Select Menu →Select and Mask →Feather: 52 → Contrast: 34 →* `OK`.
5. *Layer Menu →New →Layer Via Copy → Select Background Layer.*
6. *Filter Menu →Blur →Gaussian Blur →10 →* `OK`.
7. *Actions Pane: Stop Action* ■.
8. **Run Action on Beatles**: *File Menu →Open →C:\Data\PhotoshopCC-2\Beatles.jpg→* `Open`.

Chapter 8 - Advanced Features

9. *Select a person's head using the Elliptical Marquee Tool.*
10. *Actions Pane: Select the Blur Action → Play Selection.*

Practice Exercise 109 - Create Action2

Create an **Action** to render clouds on an image.

1. *File Menu→New→Recent Tab→Presets→Custom (7x5 in, 300 ppi, Color Mode RGB) → Create.*
2. *Window Menu→Actions Panel.*
3. *Create New Action → Name: Clouds → Record.*
4. *Choose Blue color (foreground) and White (Background) to be used as a cloud.*
5. *Filter Menu→ Render→Clouds*
6. **Actions Pane:** *Stop Playing/Recording.*
7. *File Menu→Close→Don't save the file.*
8. *File Menu→New→Recent Tab→Presets→ Custom (7x5 in, 300 ppi, Color Mode RGB) → Create.*
9. *Run the Action: Window Menu→Actions Panel→Clouds→Play Selection.*

Practice Exercise 110 - Create Action3

1. *File Tab→Open→C:\Data\PhotoshopCC-2\Fudge Almond Brownies.psd → Open.*
2. *Actions Panel→Select "Custom RGB to Grayscale" →Press the ▶ Run Button→ OK → Merge.*

8.13 Batch

This runs an **Action** on multiple files.

Practice Exercise 111 - Batch

1. **Create Action:** *File Menu→Open→C:\Data\PhotoshopCC-2\Cafe.jpg→ Open.*
2. *Actions Panel→ ⊞ Create New Action→Name: Brighten→*

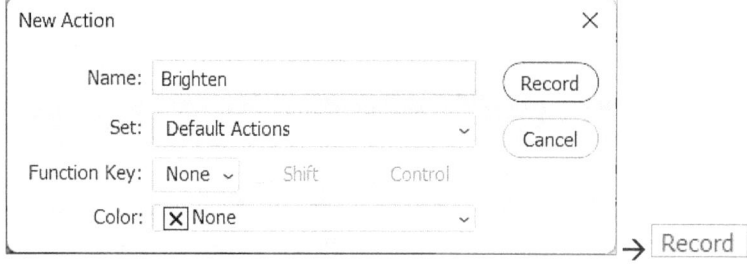

→ Record.

3. *Image Menu→ Adjustments→Brightness/Contrast→Brightness: 29→ OK.*
4. *Actions Panel→ ■ Stop Playing/Recording.*
5. **Create Batch:** *File Menu→Open→C:\Data\PhotoshopCC-2\→Using the Ctrl key select Canoe Boy.jpg, Car Hood.jpg, Family.jpg, Guitar Girl.jpg.*
6. *File Menu→Automate→Batch→(enter the following):*

Chapter 8 - Advanced Features

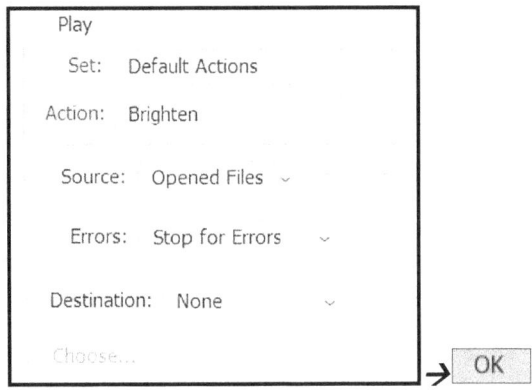

7. *Press* OK *when Complete.*

Section 3: Video Editing

You can now create and edit a **Video File** in **Photoshop**. This will allow you to place text labels (captions) and images in different positions.

8.14 Blank Video Timeline

The best way to load a **Video File** in **Photoshop** is to create a **Blank Video Timeline** and import an existing video into a **Blank Timeline.** *File Menu→New→Film & Video→Choose: Resolution Video: HDTV 1080p, 1929px X 1000 px @ 72ppi→* Create .

8.15 Motion Workspace

Motion Workspace will display a timeline and provide the video import /editing capability. *Windows Menu→Workspace→Motion.*

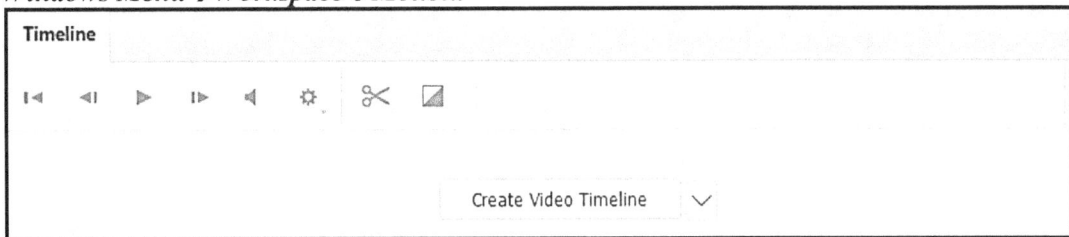

8.16 Create Video Timeline

This will create a blank **Video Timeline** (Layer 0) and a blank default **Audio Track**. *Double click on* Create Video Timeline *to create a new Video Timeline.*

Page 109

8.17 Import Video

The best way to load a **Video File** in **Photoshop** is to create a **Blank Video Timeline** and import an existing video into the **Blank Timeline**. *Press the* ✚ *(located on the right side of Layer 0)* →*File Type: Video (*.264, *3GP, *.MP4)* Video (*.264;*.3GP;*.3GPP;*.AVC;*.AVI;*.F4V;*.FLV;*.M4V;*.MOV;*.MP4;) → *C:\Data\PhotoshopCC-2\Charts.mp4* → Open . **Tip**: Use the Ctrl or Shift keys to select multiple files.

8.18 Video Group

A **Video Group** is created by default when you create a new **Blank Video Timeline** (see Layer 0 above). However, you could also place different videos or images in different groups. **To create a new Video Group:** *Press* ▯˅ *dropdown arrow (located on the left side of the default video group or Layer 0)* →*New Video Group.*

8.19 Import Image

The best way to **Import** an **Image** in a **Photoshop** timeline is to create a **New Video Group** and press the + to add an existing image. *Create a New Video Group (see above)* →*Press the* ✚ *(located on the right side of the Video Group 2)* →*File Type: JPEG (*JPG;*.JPEG;*.JPE)* → *C:\Data\PhotoshopCC-2\Alaska Island.jpg* → Open .
Tip: Use the Ctrl or Shift keys to select multiple files.

Chapter 8 - Advanced Features

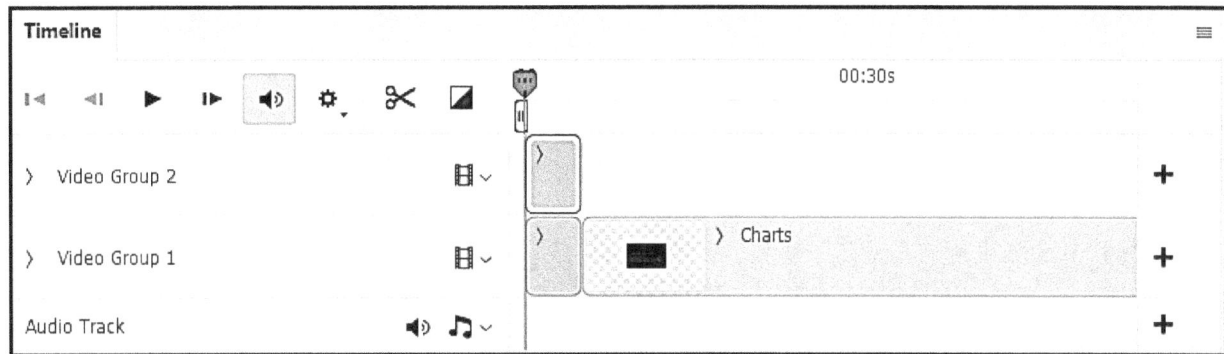

8.20 Create New Audio Track

Although you must **Import** an **Audio File** into an existing **Audio Track** a default **Auto Track** is created automatically. If you have several **Audio** files, you might want to create a separate **Audio Track** for each **Audio File**. **To create a new Audio Group:** *Press ♪˅ dropdown arrow (located on the left side of the default Audio group)→New Audio Track.*

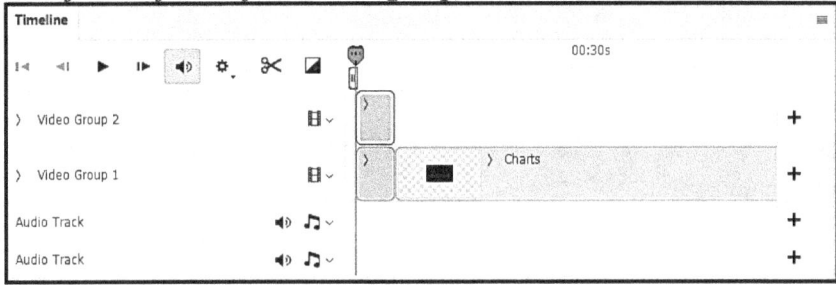

8.21 Import Audio

The best way to **Import** an existing **Audio File** is to add it to the default **Audio Track** by pressing the ✚ icon or creating a new one. *Press the ✚ (located on the right side of the Audio Track)→File Type: Audio (*.AAC;*.AC3;*.M2A;*.M4A;*.MP2;*.MP3;*.WMA;*.WM) → Jeopardyshort.mp3 →* Open . **Tip**: Use the Ctrl or Shift keys to select multiple files.

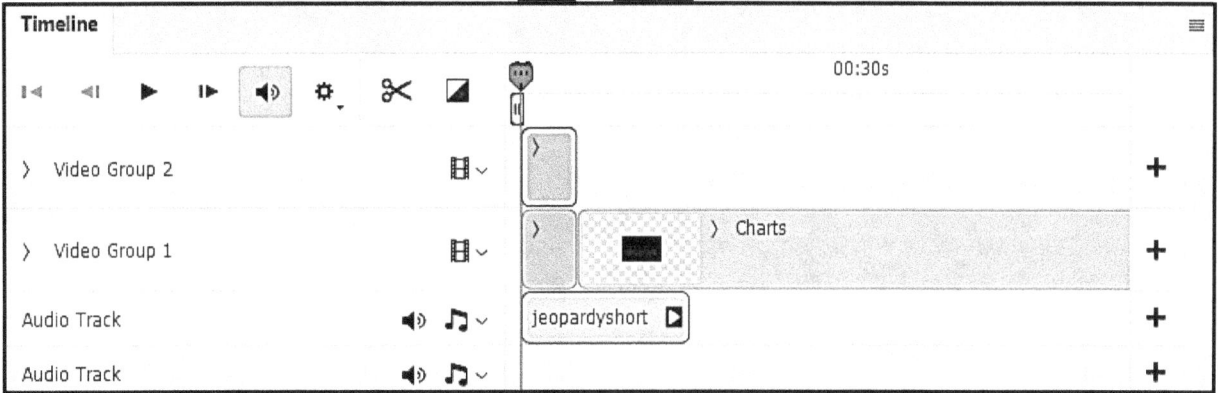

8.22 Text Captions

The best way to add a **Text Caption** is to use the T **Horizontal Type Tool** and draw a new text box for a caption. You can then automate a text box by using the **Transition** option.

T *Horizontal Type Tool→Draw a box on the screen above the Timeline.*

Chapter 8 - Advanced Features

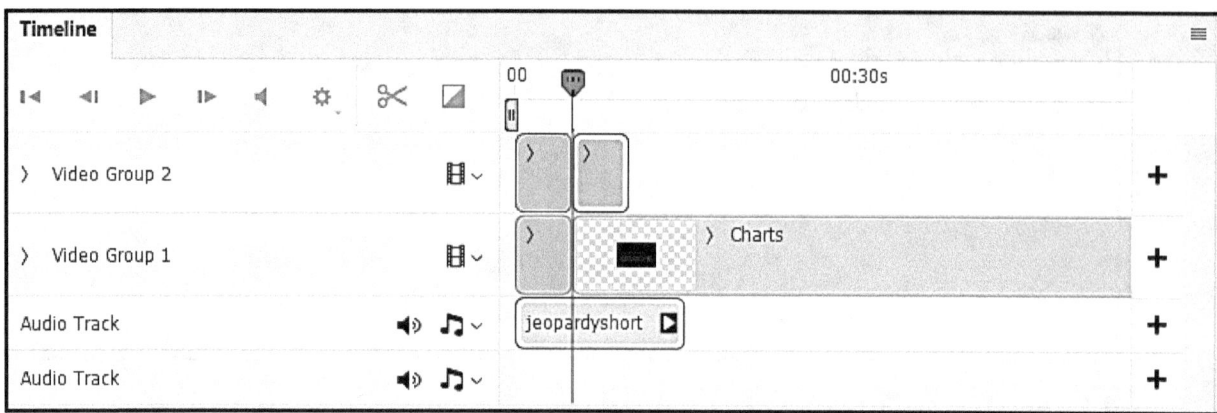

8.23 Video Tracker

This is the time position where objects will be placed. For example, if you place a **Video** in an empty location on the **Timeline** and you insert an object, it will be placed at that position. Also, the `0;00;37;21` **Time Status** will appear at the bottom of the **Timeline**.

8.24 Play Video

This will Go to the first frame, Go to the previous frame, Play video, or go to the next frame.

8.25 Audio Playback

This is an on/off switch and will **Enable audio playback** or **Mute Audio Playback** for the entire video. This can be used to temporarily mute the **Audio**.

8.26 Resolution

This will change the **Resolution** of a **Video**. The lower the **Resolution,** the better the performance.

8.27 Loop Playback

→ Loop Playback - This will **Loop** a **Video** back to the beginning.

8.28 Split At Playhead

This will cut a **Video** into two segments. It can be used to cut off and delete a segment at the beginning or end of a **Video**.

8.29 Transition

This will **Transition** a video to **Fade Out toward The End**, **Cross Fade,** **Fade With Black**, **Fade With White**, or **Fade With Color**. Also, you can specify the **Duration:** `1 s` of a **Transition**.

8.30 Convert To Frame Animation

This will convert a **Frame To Animated Gif's** that will break a video up into small **Animated GIF** clips.

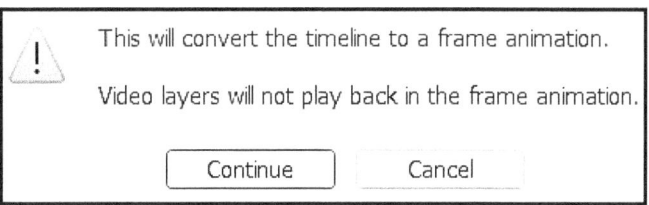

8.31 Render Video

This will convert a modified video to a new video file. **Tip**: The 📤 **Render Video** button is located at the bottom of a timeline interface. *File Menu→Export→Render Video:*

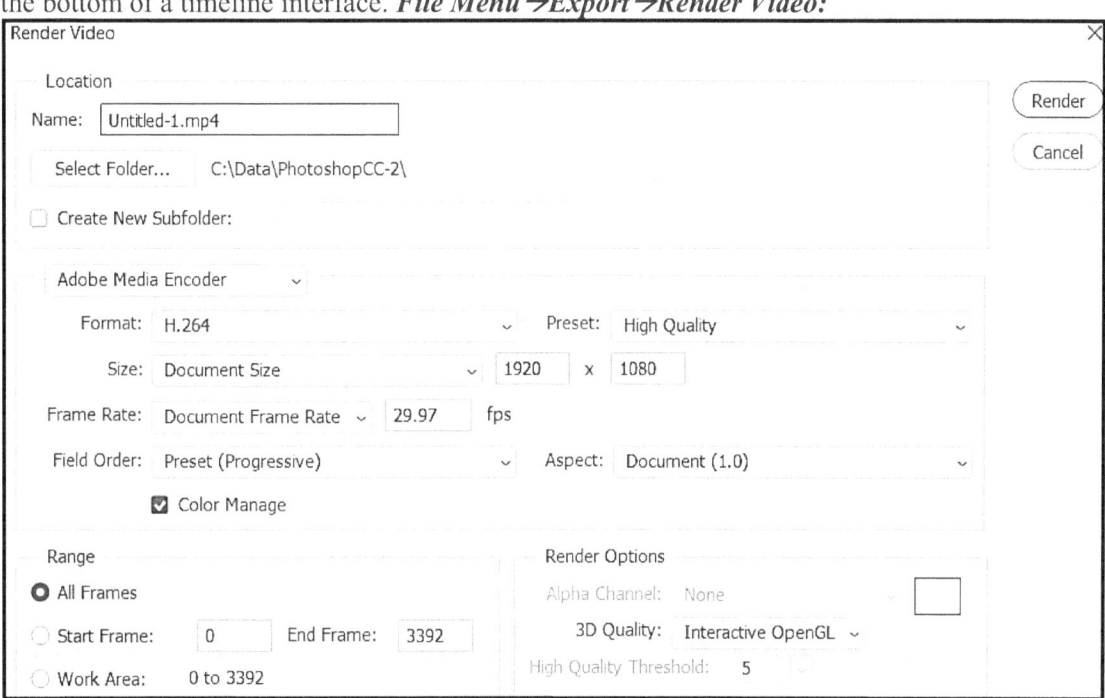

Practice Exercise 112 - Export Video

File Menu→Export→Render Video→Name: Outlook Rules1.mp4 →Render

8.32 Time Status

`0;00;37;21` This will display the position of a **Video Tracker**.

8.33 Zoom Timeline

 This will **Zoom In** or **Out** of an entire **Timeline**.

8.34 Video Layers

Each object added to a **Timeline** is created on a **New Layer**. *Windows Menu→Layers.*

Chapter 8 - Advanced Features

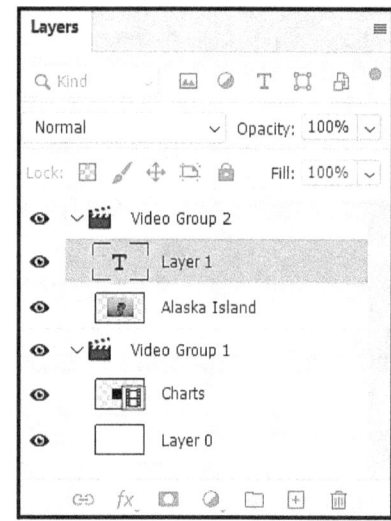

Student Project L - Edit Video

1. **Opening File:** *File Menu→Open →C:\Data\PhotoshopCC-2\Charts.mp4→* `Open`.

   Window Menu→Timeline. Place it at the bottom of the screen.
2. **Play Video:** *Play the entire video to determine where you want to edit it.*
3. **Delete Segment:** *Move the tracker to 1:00 minute. Press the scissors icon to split the video. Select the segment after the 1:00 Minute→Press the* `Delete` *key.*
4. **Adding a Caption:** *Create a new video group by selecting the drop-down arrow next to the icon→New Video Group→Horizontal Text Tool→Add a text box and type: "Enter the Data Here"→Move the text box to start at the 00:10s mark→Stretch the text box to the 00:20s mark.*

5. **Add a Logo and Place It:** *Click the drop-down arrow →Add Media→File Name: ExcelNetworks Logo.png→File of Type: PNG→* `Open`.
6. **Add Logo to a New Group:** *Click the drop-down arrow →Add Video Group→Move the logo to the New Group.*
7. *Stretch the Logo to the entire length of the video. Then, move the text field on the screen to the lower right corner by highlighting the Excel Networks bar in Video Group 3→Rectangular Marquee Tool →Draw a box around the logo→Move Tool →Move to the lower right corner.*

Chapter 8 - Advanced Features

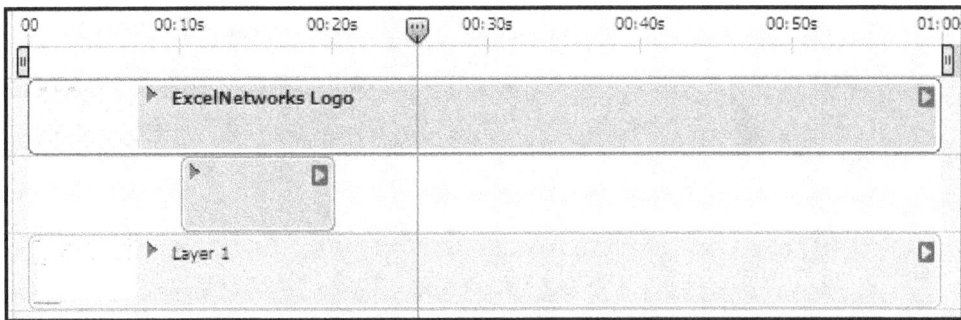

8. *Add additional captions and objects as needed to enhance the video. Create additional Video Groups* ▣⁃ *to see if objects appear at the same time. To change the measurement from frames to seconds: Change the status bar to "Document Sizes."*

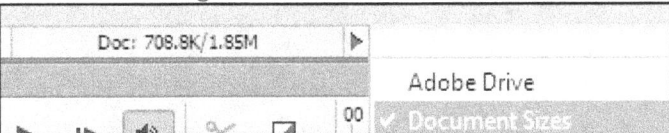

Section 4: 3D Object Manipulation

8.35 3D Tools

This feature is available in the **Photoshop CS6 Extended Version**. (*Help →About Photoshop*). It has been drastically improved over **Photoshop CS5**.

Practice Exercise 113 - 3D Tools

1. *File Menu→New→ Print Tab →Print Presets →Letter (8.5 x 11 in @ 300 ppi →* `Create`.
2. *Text Tool* T *→Type: 3D→Font size: 100 pts.*
3. *Select the text layer →3D Menu → New 3D Extrusion from Selected Layer →Move 3D cursor to create the 3D object →3D Menu → Render. Tip: This process could take a long time. Click on the screen to stop rendering, and (3D Menu →Resume Render) to continue.*

Before Rendering:  **After Rendering**:

8.36 3D Axis

When you click on the 🖩 icon in the **3D Ribbon** (*Window Menu →3D*), an axis will appear that allows you to rotate the object in 3 dimensions.

Index - Touch-Up And Image Adjustments

3D Tools ...115
Actions ...107
Add Anchor Point Tool ...92
Alignment ...54
Art History Brush Tool ...26
Auto Color ...60
Auto Contrast ...60
Auto Tone ...60
Background ...51
Background Eraser Tool ...23
Batch ...108
Bicubic ...58
Black and White ...66
Blur Tool ...41
Brightness/Contrast ...60
Brush Defaults ...33
Brush Tool ...10
Burn Tool ...44
Channel Mixer ...68
Character Panel ...89
Clipping Mask ...84
Clone Stamp Tool ...39
Color Balance ...66
Color Lookup ...69
Color Replacement Tool ...21
Color Sampler Tool ...25
Content-Aware Fill ...86
Content-Aware Move Tool 86
Content-Aware Scale ...86
Convert Point Tool ...92
Convert Smart Object ...52
Count Tool ...31
Create Custom Patterns ...29
Crop Tool ...35
Curves ...63
Custom Shape Tool ...17
Delete Anchor Point ...92
Desaturate ...73
Direct Selection Tool ...93
Document Size ...56
Dodge Tool ...43
Edit Smart Object ...52
Ellipse Tool ...17
Equalize ...75
Eraser Tool ...14
Export Video Files ...113

Exposure ...64
Eye Dropper Tool ...9
Filter Effects ...6
Freeform Tool ...91
General Drawing Tools ...8
Gradient Map ...70
Gradient Tool ...27
Hand Tool ...20
HDR Toning ...72
Healing Brush Tool ...37
Hide Selection ...83
History Brush Tool ...13
Horizontal Type Tool ...16
Hue/Saturation ...65
Image Adjustments ...55, 59
Image Compression ...58
Image Resolution ...55
Index Layers ...51
Invert ...69
Layer Adjustments ...50
Layer Blending Modes ...48
Layer Comps ...94
Layer Effects ...6
Layer Fill ...49
Layer Filter ...47
Layer Locked ...49
Layer Mask ...49
Layer New Group ...53
Layer Opacity ...49
Layer Panel Menu ...53
Layer Style ...49
Layer Visibility ...50
Layers ...6
Levels ...61
Mac vs Windows ...5
Magic Eraser Tool ...31
Match Color ...73
Mixer Brush ...22
Move Tool ...8
New Layer ...50
Non-Destructive Image Adjustments ...59
Note Tool ...30
Paint Bucket Tool ...15
Panels ...6
Paragraph Panel ...90

Patch Tool ...38
Path Selection Tool ...92
Pattern Stamp Tool ...28
Pencil Tool ...12
Photo Filter ...68
Photoshop Environment ...5
Pin Tool ...91
Pixel Dimension ...55
Polygon Tool ...17
Posterize ...69
Puppet Warp Tool ...87
Quick Mask Background Color ...82
Quick Mask Painting ...81
Raster Layers ...51
Rectangle Tool ...17
Redeye Tool ...39
Replace Color ...74
Resolution type ...6
Reveal Selection ...82
Rounded Rectangle Tool .17
Ruler Tool ...30
Saving Techniques ...6
Selective Color ...70
Shadows/Highlights ...71
Shape Layers ...51
Shape Tools ...17
Sharpen Tool ...42
Slice Select Tool ...32
Slice Tool ...32
Smart Object Embedded .51
Smart Object Linked ...52
Smudge Tool ...42
Sponge Tool ...44
Spot Healing Brush Tool ...36
Text Layer Effects ...89
Text Layers ...51
Threshold ...70
Trash Layer ...50
Vanishing Point ...95
Vibrance ...65
Video Files ...109
Wrap text on a path ...93
Zooming ...5

Detailed Table Of Contents

Chapter 1 - Quick Review 5
    1.1 Exercises 5
    1.2 Mac Keyboard Commands 5
    1.3 Photoshop Environment 5
    1.4 Zooming 5
    1.5 Panels 6
    1.6 Basic Drawing Tools 6
    1.7 Resolution Type 6
    1.8 Selection 6
    1.9 Layers 6
    1.10 Filter Effects 6
    1.11 Layer Effects 6
    1.12 Saving Techniques 6
    1.13 Duplicate Layers 7
    1.14 Help Tools 7
    1.15 Color Picker 7

Chapter 2 - In-Depth Drawing Tools 8
    Section 1: Core Tools 8
        2.1 Move Tool 8
        2.2 Eye Dropper Tool 9
        2.3 Brush Tool 10
        2.4 Pencil Tool 12
        2.5 History Brush Tool 13
        2.6 Eraser Tool 14
        2.7 Paint Bucket Tool 15
        2.8 Horizontal Type Tool 16
        2.9 Shape Tools 17
        2.10 Hand Tool 20
    Section 2: Optional Tools 21
        2.11 Color Replacement Tool 21
        2.12 Mixer Brush Tool 22
        2.13 Background Eraser Tool 23
        2.14 Color Sampler Tool 25
        2.15 Art History Brush Tool 26
        2.16 Gradient Tool 27
        2.17 Pattern Stamp Tool 28
        2.18 Create Custom Patterns 29
        2.19 Ruler Tool 30
        2.20 Note Tool 30
        2.21 Count Tool 31
        2.22 Magic Eraser Tool 31
        2.23 Slice Tool 32
        2.24 Slice Select Tool 32
        2.25 Brush Defaults 33
        2.26 Add New Brushes 34
        2.27 Create New Brushes 34

Chapter 3 - Touch-Up Images 35
    3.1 Crop Tool 35

Detailed Table Of Contents

    3.2 Spot Healing Brush Tool 36
    3.3 Healing Brush Tool 37
    3.4 Patch Tool 38
    3.5 Redeye Tool 39
    3.6 Clone Stamp Tool 39
    3.7 Blur Tool 41
    3.8 Sharpen Tool 42
    3.9 Smudge Tool 42
    3.10 Dodge Tool 43
    3.11 Burn Tool 44
    3.12 Sponge Tool 44

Chapter 4 - Advanced Layers **47**
  Section 1: Layer Panel Options 47
    4.1 Layer Filter 47
    4.2 Layer Blending Modes 48
    4.3 Opacity 49
    4.4 Fill 49
    4.5 Locked Layer 49
    4.6 Layer Style 49
    4.7 Layer Mask 49
    4.8 Layer Adjustments 50
    4.9 New Layer 50
    4.10 Trash Can 50
  Section 2: Visible Layers 50
    4.11 Layer Visibility 50
    4.12 Background Layer 51
    4.13 Raster Layers 51
    4.14 Shape Layers 51
    4.15 Text Layers 51
    4.16 Index Layers 51
    4.17 Smart Object 51
  Section 3: Layer Menu 53
    4.18 New Group 53
    4.19 Link Layer 53
    4.20 Merge Down 53
    4.21 Merge Visible 53
    4.22 Flatten Image 53
    4.23 Panel Options 53
  Section 4: Layer Manipulation 54
    4.24 Alignment 54
    4.25 Distribute 54
    4.26 Layer Via Copy 54
    4.27 Layer Via Cut 54
    4.28 Layer 54
    4.29 Duplicate Layer 54
    4.30 Delete Layer 54
    4.31 Rasterize 54

Chapter 5 - Image Adjustments **55**
  Section 1: Canvas and Image Size Adjustments 55
    5.1 Image Size 55
    5.2 Canvas Size 56

Detailed Table Of Contents

    5.3 Image Compression 58
  Section 2: Image Adjustments 59
    5.4 Auto Tone 60
    5.5 Auto Contrast 60
    5.6 Auto Color 60
    5.7 Brightness/Contrast 60
    5.8 Levels 61
    5.9 Curves 63
    5.10 Exposure 64
  Section 3: Color Adjustments 64
    5.11 Vibrance 65
    5.12 Hue/Saturation 65
    5.13 Color Balance 66
    5.14 Black & White 66
    5.15 Photo Filter 68
    5.16 Channel Mixer 68
    5.17 Color Lookup 69
  Section 4: Color Replacement Adjustment 69
    5.18 Invert 69
    5.19 Posterize 69
    5.20 Threshold 70
    5.21 Gradient Map 70
    5.22 Selective Color 70
  Section 5: Toning Adjustments 71
    5.23 Shadows/Highlights 71
    5.24 HDR Toning 72
  Section 6: Other Color Adjustments 73
    5.25 Desaturate 73
    5.26 Match Color 73
    5.27 Replace Color 74
    5.28 Equalize 75

Chapter 6 - Masking Capabilities **77**
  Section 1: Select and Mask 77
    6.1 Select and Mask Button 77
    6.2 Drawing Adjustment Tools 77
    6.3 Background Overlays 78
    6.4 View Mode 78
    6.5 Refine Mode 79
    6.6 Edge Detection 79
    6.7 Global Refinement 79
    6.8 Output Settings 79
  Section 2: Quick Mask 81
    6.9 Quick Mask Painting 81
    6.10 Quick Mask Background Color 82
  Section 3: Layer Mask 82
    6.11 Reveal Selection 82
    6.12 Hide Selection 83
    6.13 Replace Sky 83
  Section 4: Clipping Mask 84
    6.14 Clipping Mask 84
  Section 5: Advanced Techniques 86

Detailed Table Of Contents

    6.15 Content-Aware Scale 86
    6.16 Content-Aware Move Tool 86
    6.17 Content-Aware Fill 86
    6.18 Puppet Warp Tool 87

Chapter 7 - Text Layer Effects 89
  Section 1: Text Formatting 89
    7.1 Type Options 89
    7.2 Character Panel 89
    7.3 Paragraph Panel 90
    7.4 Transform Text Box 91
  Section 2: Reshape Text Path 91
    7.5 Pen Tool 91
    7.6 Freeform Tool 91
    7.7 Add Anchor Point Tool 92
    7.8 Delete Anchor Point Tool 92
    7.9 Convert Point Tool 92
    7.10 Path Selection Tool 92
    7.11 Direct Selection Tool 93
    7.12 Warp Text Options Bar 93
    7.13 Warp Text 93
  Section 3: Layer Comps 94
    7.14 Layer Comps 94
  Section 4: Vanishing Point 95
    7.15 Vanishing Point 95

Chapter 8 - Advanced Features 97
  Section 1: Neural Filters 97
    8.1 Skin Smoothing 97
    8.2 Smart Portrait 98
    8.3 Makeup Transfer 99
    8.4 Landscape Mixer 100
    8.5 Style Transfer 100
    8.6 Harmonize 101
    8.7 Color Transfer 103
    8.8 Colorize 103
    8.9 Super Zoom 104
    8.10 Depth Blur 105
    8.11 JPEG Artifacts Removal 106
  Section 2: Actions 107
    8.12 Actions 107
    8.13 Batch 108
  Section 3: Video Editing 109
    8.14 Blank Video Timeline 109
    8.15 Motion Workspace 109
    8.16 Create Video Timeline 109
    8.17 Import Video 110
    8.18 Video Group 110
    8.19 Import Image 110
    8.20 Create New Audio Track 111
    8.21 Import Audio 111
    8.22 Text Captions 111
    8.23 Video Tracker 112

Detailed Table Of Contents

    8.24 Play Video 112
    8.25 Audio Playback 112
    8.26 Resolution 112
    8.27 Loop Playback 112
    8.28 Split At Playhead 112
    8.29 Transition 112
    8.30 Convert To Frame Animation 112
    8.31 Render Video 113
    8.32 Time Status 113
    8.33 Zoom Timeline 113
    8.34 Video Layers 113
  Section 4: 3D Object Manipulation 115
    8.35 3D Tools 115
    8.36 3D Axis 115
Index - Touch-Up And Image Adjustments 117
Detailed Table Of Contents 118

Adobe Courseware
Step-By-Step Training Guides and Workbooks
Available on Amazon.com (Search for author, Jeff Hutchinson)

To review a sample book, see the sample video clip, and Amazon reviews, and to purchase: Go To: https://www.elearnlogic.com. These **Step-By-Step Training Guides** focus on specific learning concepts including brief descriptions as well as many short 2-5 minute exercises for practice. The Table of Contents and Index will allow students to look up desired concepts quickly and easily. These guides are invaluable resources used to build and maintain computer skills for industry, as well as for personal use.

Available in Paperback: $9.95 or Kindle eBook: $5.95

https://www.amazon.com/dp/1976401321 https://www.amazon.com/dp/1976401607 https://www.amazon.com/dp/1976466695 https://www.amazon.com/dp/1976467004

About the Author
Jeff Hutchinson is a corporate computer trainer and consultant. He teaches **Microsoft** and **Adobe** products from beginning to advanced topics. Jeff has a BS degree from BYU in Computer-Aided

https://www.amazon.com/dp/1987724038

Engineering and owned a computer training and consulting firm in San Francisco, California for several years. He currently works as an independent

Contact Information: Jeff Hutchinson, jeffhutch@elearnlogic.com or (801) 376-6687.

Evaluation copy: http://www.elearnlogic.com/